Athene Series
Feminist Scholarship on Culture and Education

Women in Power
Pathways to Leadership in Education
Barbara Curry

Pioneering Deans of Women
More Than Wise and Pious Matrons
Jana Nidiffer

"Stalwart Women"
A Historical Analysis of Deans of Women in the South
Carolyn Terry Bashaw

Pedagogies of Resistance
Women Educator Activists, 1880–1960
Margaret Smith Crocco, Petra Munro, & Kathleen Weiler

The *Feminist Teacher* Anthology
Pedagogies and Classroom Strategies
Gail E. Cohee, Elisabeth Däumer, Theresa D. Kemp, Paula M. Krebs, Sue Lafky, & Sandra Runzo, Editors

Feminist Science Education
Angela Calabrese Barton

Disciplining Sexuality
Foucault, Life Histories, and Education
Sue Middleton

Privilege in the Medical Academy
A Feminist Examines Gender, Race, and Power
Delese Wear

Re-Engineering Female Friendly Science
Sue V. Rosser

All the Rage
Reasserting Radical Lesbian Feminism
Lynne Harne & Elaine Miller, Editors

Creating an Inclusive College Curriculum
A Teaching Sourcebook from the New Jersey Project
Ellen G. Friedman, Wendy K. Kolmar, Charley B. Flint, and Paula Rothenberg, Editors

Teaching the Majority
Breaking the Gender Barrier in Science, Mathematics, and Engineering
Sue V. Rosser, Editor

The Will to Violence
The Politics of Personal Behavior
Susanne Kappeler

Crucial Conversations
Interpreting Contemporary American Literary Autobiographies by Women
Jeanne Braham

Women's Studies Graduates
The First Generation
Barbara F. Luebke & Mary Ellen Reilly

Men Who Control Women's Health
The Miseducation of Obstetrician-Gynecologists
Diana Scully

The Transsexual Empire
The Making of the She-Male
Janice G. Raymond

Surviving the Dalkon Shield IUD
Women v. the Pharmaceutical Industry
Karen Hicks

Making Violence Sexy
Feminist Views on Pornography
Diana E. H. Russell, Editor

Father Knows Best
The Use and Abuse of Power in Freud's Case of Dora
Robin Tolmach Lakoff & James C. Coyne

Living by the Pen
Early British Women Writers
Dale Spender, Editor

The Knowledge Explosion
Generations of Feminist Scholarship
Cheris Kramarae & Dale Spender, Editors

All Sides of the Subject
Women and Biography
Teresa Iles, Editor

Calling the Equality Bluff
Women in Israel
Barbara Swirski & Marilyn P. Safir, Editors

Black Feminist Criticism
Perspectives on Black Women Writers
Barbara Christian

Narodniki Women
Russian Women Who Sacrificed Themselves for the Dream of Freedom
Margaret Maxwell

Speaking Freely
Unlearning the Lies of the Fathers' Tongues
Julia Penelope

(continued)

ATHENE SERIES *(continued)*

The Reflowering of the Goddess
Gloria Feman Orenstein

Female-Friendly Science
Applying Women's Studies Methods and Theories to Attract Students
Sue V. Rosser

The Sexual Liberals and the Attack on Feminism
Dorchen Leidholdt & Janice G. Raymond, Editors

Between Worlds
Women Writers of Chinese Ancestry
Amy Ling

Whence the Goddesses
A Source Book
Miriam Robbins Dexter

Made to Order
The Myth of Reproductive and Genetic Progress
Patricia Spallone & Deborah Lynn Steinberg, Editors

Exposing Nuclear Phallacies
Diana E. H. Russell, Editor

Teaching Science and Health from a Feminist Perspective
A Practical Guide
Sue V. Rosser

Taking Our Time
Feminist Perspectives on Temporality
Frieda Johles Forman & Caoran Sowton, Editors

Educating for Peace
A Feminist Perspective
Birgit Brock-Utne

Men's Studies Modified
The Impact of Feminism on the Academic Disciplines
Dale Spender, Editor

Stopping Rape
Successful Survival Strategies
Pauline B. Bart & Patricia H. O'Brien

Feminism Within the Science and Health Care Professions
Overcoming Resistance
Sue V. Rosser, Editor

Feminist Perspectives on Peace and Peace Education
Birgit Brock-Utne

Feminist Approaches to Science
Ruth Bleier, Editor

Science and Gender
A Critique of Biology and Its Theories on Women
Ruth Bleier

WOMEN IN POWER

Pathways to Leadership in Education

BARBARA K. CURRY
Foreword by Maxine Greene

TEACHERS COLLEGE
COLUMBIA UNIVERSITY
NEW YORK AND LONDON

Published by Teachers College Press, 1234 Amsterdam Avenue, New York, NY 10027

Copyright © 2000 by Teachers College, Columbia University

Library of Congress Cataloging-in-Publication Data

Curry, Barbara K.
    Women in power : pathways to leadership in education / by Barbara Curry ; foreword by Maxine Greene.
        p. cm. — (Athene series)
    Includes bibliographical references (p.) and index.
    ISBN 0-8077-3911-1 (cloth : alk. paper) — ISBN 0-8077-3910-3 (pbk. : alk. paper)
        1. Women school administrators—United States.   2. Women educators—United States.   3. Educational leadership—United States.
    I. Title.   II. Series.
LB2831.62.C87 2000
    371.2'011'082—dc21   99-049364

ISBN 0-8077-3910-3 (paper)
ISBN 0-8077-3911-1 (cloth)

Printed on acid-free paper
Manufactured in the United States of America

07 06 05 04 03 02 01 00   8 7 6 5 4 3 2 1

To the women of my family.

Most especially

to my mother Carolyn Katherine Curry
and my niece Kellee Anne Brown

Contents

Foreword *by Maxine Greene*   ix

Introduction: Making Our Way Through Life   1

1. Classic Representations of Leadership   **5**

Task-Related Discussions of Leadership   6
Power Differentials and Egalitarianism   8
Great Men and Mythical Leaders   10
Attributes, Personal Characteristics, and Character Traits   12
Comparisons of Men and Women Leaders   14
An Emerging Approach to Leadership   16

**2. A Framework for Analysis of
the Leader Persona**   **20**

The Leader Persona and Individual Identity   21
A Theory of Leader Identity Development   27
Women's Construction of Their Leader Persona   29
Achieving the Truce   40

**3. The Confluence of Past Experiences
and Present Circumstances**   **43**

Identity Development Through Maturation   44
Leader Pathways Through Psychosocial Development   47
The Significance of Defining Experiences on the
     Leader Identity   50
Individuals and Leaders as Socially Constructed   59

4. Transcendent Themes and the Leader Persona **64**

Transcendent Themes 66

Transcendent Themes and Instrumentation in the
Process of Leading 84

**5. The Esthetics of the Leader Persona and
the Practice of Proaction and Self-Study** **86**

The Esthetics of the Leader Persona Defined 87

The Convergence of Conferred Identity and
Professional Constructions 88

Phenomenological Epistemological Processes 89

The Influence of Social Contexts on the Emergence
of the Leader Esthetics 91

The Fusion of Social Contexts 94

Proaction in the Design of the Leader Persona 98

Toward Developing a Practice of Proaction and Self-Study 101

References 103

Index 107

About the Author 111

Foreword

When the literature on moral development was shown by Carol Gilligan and others to have dealt only with male subjects, many of us in education were astonished. Likewise—given the number of women teachers in the schools, especially—we found it hard to believe that the best-known and most highly regarded psychologists had relied exclusively on masculine norms when they studied patterns of responsibility and leadership in schools. As in the case of studies on moral development, scholars recognized the importance of relationship, but nevertheless gave highest priority to autonomy, self-reliance, individuation, and natural rights. *Women in Power: Pathways to Leadership in Education* sheds a strong light on this imbalance of emphasis in the literature on leadership.

The author here is concerned with what it means to be presented only with male role models when women attempt to construct themselves as leaders in their particular fields. Dr. Barbara Curry highlights this difficulty by reminding us of the figures that have become icons for men (and, in turn, for society as a whole): heroic and dominating figures, mythic images, embodiments of power. Women struggling to construct themselves as leaders have to cope with popular images of vulnerability, self-mastery, and a distinctively male confidence. District superintendents very often keep alive memories of stern fathers, whose authority was not to be denied. Not only do would-be women leaders have to cope with the persistent images of male dominance; the only professional literature available to the women trying to master what is demanded of contemporary leadership consists largely of information gathered by male policy-makers, presumed experts in theories of leadership, and male administrators on many levels of the schools.

Barbara Curry takes a well-honed constructivist approach to all of this. One of the important definitions of constructivist leadership that enables the members of an educational community to construct meanings and, in time, a common purpose, has to do with reciprocity. Reciprocity, mutuality, connectedness: these are among the watchwords when it comes to women's leadership and the ways in which women construct themselves as leaders. As is well known, however, hierarchy and bureaucracy still mark most school and school districts, and we cannot but be struck by the ways in which male leaders have managed to accommodate themselves to structures of that sort. It may be that the constructivist perspectives that mark the writing and the schoolroom praxis of more and more women may lead to fundamental transformations of the schools. Teamwork, collaboration, conversation: women working to create what are called their "personae" as leaders may bring about notable changes, not only in their own contexts but in the larger contexts of American education.

To take a constructivist approach to becoming a leader inevitably involves a person's consideration of her identity. This book focuses centrally on the problem of identity, for all its careful attention to theory making and empirical study. Readers may be reminded of John Dewey, writing that "the self is not ready-made, but something in formation through choice of action. . . ." Like certain existential thinkers (Camus, for instance, or Sartre) Dewey believed that the self—the identity—is formed through interest in a particular project or way of being in the work. Many of us in education can recall shaping our identities (as teachers, as students, perhaps as principals) by means of a concrete project. Barbara Curry emphasizes the need to invent a *persona* that enables one to make herself present to the world in response to the demands of the workplace, the school, the district office, even the state or federal agency.

This book reaches an apex when addressing identity and its relation to the construction of the self as leader. Much is made clear when the author draws our attention to eight women, each of whom we come to know through her biographical narratives. Dr. Curry shares with us her approach to interviewing that she shares with Mary Belenky and her colleagues, authors of *Women's Ways of Knowing*. Aspects of a new epistemology, a feminist-influenced way of knowing, make the construction of the selves that arouse our interest become dramatic in their difference and complexity. There is no question but that much of the importance of this book stems from the direct contact we experience by means of the interviews with these distinctive women. Each of them has evolved to become a leader, through a long exertion of effort without the mentoring (or a version of the "old boys' club") enjoyed by so many of her male colleagues. It is indeed a matter of courageously and intelligently constructing oneself as a leader or as a leader-to-be in a not-always-hospitable world. The stories to which Dr. Curry introduces us shed light (as qualitative research is always likely to do) on the theoretical and empirical sections of the text. Many readers may find themselves newly aroused to seek out roads not yet traveled, largely because of the questions raised. Dr. Curry's own wide range of knowledge, and the histories lived by individual women are challenging us with a new perspective on leadership, responsive to the unpredictable shifts and changes in a postmodern world.

Maxine Greene
Teachers College
Columbia University

WOMEN IN POWER

Pathways to Leadership in Education

Introduction:
Making Our Way Through Life

There seems to be in each of us a novice who is most acutely aware of the metaphorical walk forward in the direction of a destiny. That part of us, in our youth, often moves toward the future with anticipation of success and with trepidation.

As a young woman out of high school and looking earnestly for a sense of myself in the future, I joined a consciousness-raising group at a local women's center. Similar centers were cropping up as sources of support for individuals like myself at the time. During an early session, those of us attending were introducing ourselves and including a brief statement of our reasons for coming to the group.

I began my statement characteristically, for that period in my life, by providing a litany of experiences that I believed were particularly brutal and, of course, potentially defining. Wanting to offer the women an ending to my introduction that was a bit more upbeat, I concluded by saying that I was in the process of becoming. My pronouncement was well received—so much so that I felt flattered and believed that being the only African American in the room was not a problem or a source of grief. I found that the women in the group I had joined were on a quest, attempting to be something other than the sum of their socialization up to that period in their lives.

That socialization made us followers. As such we were taught to give into subjugation by our parents (in particular by our mothers) and to serve our fathers, our lovers, our husbands, and our sons. I expected to be subservient to the object of my love. All of my romantic fantasies were of that nature. They were also improbable, in retrospect. On the one hand, I was always too stubborn to be a servant; on the other, there were few men living at the time who would go against their own socialization to accept a nonservile black woman. Also, at the time the only role models for men of color who might be able to subjugate me were Native Americans in cowboy films—or "shoot-em-ups" as my father referred to them. African-American men were portrayed without dignity or virility. My father as a role model did not surface in my psyche until much later in my life. I did eventually experience him in different men of different races. The endings of those relationships were always the same: I extricated myself. And I did so in the absence of the confidence I needed to believe I was right. Consequently, I suffered.

The role of mother as servant to her son was a secret revelation to me at the time. Until the revelation, I believed that motherhood preempted such servitude. Although I had observed the mother-servant, I assumed it was an anomalous behavior in response to misbehaving children. Perhaps I did not expect to be a servant because I had no brothers to observe in relation to my mother.

The women in the group, myself included, were followers who were attempting to become self-directed and, as such, leaders. Nevertheless, we had aspirations of one kind or another. The common theme was to gain control of our lives, including our relationships and our careers. It seemed that we wanted very much to celebrate the changes we were working to achieve. Indeed, coming together and celebrating were parts of an unarticulated right of passage. We were changing ourselves from girls, even though we were of varying ages. Although there were grandmothers among us, movement from girls to women was our intended direction. The vehicle, the consciousness-raising group offered at the women's center, was to serve as our transaction process and a place for our metamorphoses.

The discussion begun in a room might easily spill over into an extended exchange by telephone, over a luncheon, or into a happy hour late on a Friday afternoon. The prelude to parting was a hug accompanied by encouragement. We were brave-hearted individuals. We each held a post as sage regarding some aspect of our lives. As such, we applied healing poultices to the wounds of our kindred. Our dilemma: not being followers made us feel badly. It was as if we had failed or were failing at something significant in our lives—perhaps at achieving our destinies, which were dictated in a very masculine world at the time. We were bad girls in the early days of our transformation. The urge to be good girls was daunting—made us weak and unable to be anything that resembled overt bravery. Instead we had to be beguiling. It stayed with us like an addiction to an opiate, through our anger, tears, and joy. As we predicted for ourselves, the guilt we felt from daring to be different remained throughout our attempts to gain clarification and serenity.

Some of us declared ourselves to be "bad with abandonment." We knew what it meant to be bad. The phrase was based on culturally embedded beliefs that self-directedness and leadership were unacceptable for our gender. It included any inclination we might have to define ourselves in ways that could be constructed as duplicitous, given the expectation that we were to follow a male partner throughout our lives. "Bad" referred to the necessity for men to accommodate such willfulness.

Since my experience in the group, I have found that little girls are still raised to be followers for the most part. There are always exceptions, and I might offer up a "thank-you" to those parents who went against the grain by instilling in their daughters expectations of achievement and proaction.

For women, leadership studies have largely told us how to rise above our circumstances, to rise above being women, in order to apply prescriptive behaviors. The value in the most demanding of organizational exchanges is a woman's ability to anticipate and mimic a masculine response. It is therefore reasonable that women ascending to leadership positions find themselves acutely aware of their own evolution, changing psychology, and immersion in old conflicts as the work of becoming is added to the burden of legitimizing their position among their followers. The point is that it does not require an extraordinary imagination to crystallize the image of woman as leader within conventions of feminism.

As I suggested earlier, to view myself and other women in unconventional roles is more difficult; women as leaders have been described as exceptional. While I am reluctant to make predictions, I am even more reluctant to suggest that any one of the women in the group had reached, or would eventually attain, a perfect state of maturation—whatever that is.

It was apparent to us that no particular combination of experiences could be liberating in absolute terms. It also seemed to us that our destinies could very well involve a lifetime of trial and error, with the possibility of our future decisions about our lives being based on the enlightenment we expected to enjoy as we grew older. If we were not about to undergo a dramatic, life-altering transformation, then why did we gather each week—and for several years, in some cases? We came together for the company, for empathy, for mentoring, and for witnesses to our transformation. We thought that we could serve these purposes for each other. Over the years the group has become a network of friendships. And the naiveté of youth has given way to more narrowly focused life purposes.

I recall that the more global aspirations of the group included the normalization of the success of women rather than the maintenance of its exceptionality. However, in many instances a woman as leader remains an exception. Our most celebrated achievements still focus on our ability to follow. In this discussion I have attempted to explore the idea of women as leaders in less conventional ways. As such, I have steered clear of prescribing kinds of leadership. This includes acquiring behaviors typically viewed as masculine or aggressive. Masculinizing women's work attire has been a signal of this approach as the power suit of the 1980s symbolizes. It was testosterone applied topically. There are volumes that offer this important focus on instrumentation. I have attempted to chart a course beyond characterizations of leadership that have been staples in readings for the novice. I refer to these as the classical representation of leadership. These classics serve as grounding for anyone who is interested in exploring early discussions on the topic.

In the following discussion I consider women as leaders on their own terms. This necessarily involves the kinds of conflicts that often accompany their ascendency to such positions, including the questions of identity, balancing socially constructed and normalized roles and responsibilities, and the issue of marginality both in their professions and in the public mind. I hope the contribution of this discussion will be the consideration of leadership through the lenses of adult identity development. To do this, I borrow heavily from theorists and researchers in the field in order to achieve several contextual goals. The first, after providing background in the conventional approaches to the subject (classical approaches), is to provide a conceptual framework for linking adult development with the leader persona. The second is to explore individuals' pathways through sociocultural and psychosocial terrains to their ascendency to leadership positions. The third is to consider proaction in development of a constellation of features of identity that are brought to bear on leadership practice. I have also attempted to avoid prescribing pathways toward development of that constellation which I refer to as an aspect of leader identity and the leader persona.

As I suggested earlier, my concern in building this discussion has been to replace regimented and prescribed leadership with a phenomenological approach. In this way, leadership and becoming a leader is a fluid, adaptive process oriented toward individual development. The cases incorporated into this discussion are company for a journey, in the same way the consciousness-raising groups were for the women attending them. Our journey through life is a personal one. Our pathways through life are illuminated by retrospectives, as is this text. I am grateful to the women mentioned in this discussion for sharing parts of their lives and allowing me to place them like sketches, albeit incomplete, herein.

1

Classic Representations of Leadership

"Characterizations of leadership have been variable, and definitions of 'good' have been vague even though the two have always gone together on the page, in the literature, and finally as part of an organization's survival code."

We generally think of organizations as social structures that have among their primary responsibilities the construction and exchange of ideas. The quality of those creative processes as well as their outcomes affect whether or not organizations are recognized and understood as functional and productive. To be described as such is most desirable. The contrary is easily problematic, signaling the disintegration or the end of the structure. Like the people who make them up, organizations come in varying shapes and sizes and can be sorted along a continuum, plotting their internal state. They are neither dichotomous nor oppositional, neither highly functional nor dysfunctional; rather they are some portion of each, with the ratio determining their longevity as well as their productivity.

We seldom, if ever, view an organization's stabilization at a midpoint as an occasion to talk about its leadership unless that stability is also viewed as stagnation or resistance to change—particularly after the need to change has been foreshadowed. Leadership is the focus of assessment during an organization's early developmental phases and toward the end of the consolidation of its structure. Consequently, we celebrate an organization's beginning and eulogize its ending. For those of us who have not been through too many of them, we anticipate restructurings. We energize ourselves for renewal and rebirth. We anticipate the organization's beginning and our place in that new community. In some instances, for stockholders and stakeholders (employees) alike, restructurings may well fulfill all of their hopes.

What is new and right, and what is problematic and wrong, is laid at the feet of the organization's leader. The panacea for the ailing organization is "good leadership." This may be as well known and practical as the prescription "starve a fever and feed a cold"—or vice versa, depending on the culture in which we find ourselves.

Comments to and about leaders are telling, ranging from a list of outstanding accomplishments and "sorry you are choosing to move on" to complaints about job performance and "sorry but you really must leave for the good of the cause." The "cause," of course, is survival. Characterizations of leadership have varied, and definitions of *good* have been vague, even though the two have always gone together on the page, in the literature, and finally as part of an organization's survival code.

Leadership has been defined in ways that are task-related, that cover themes of egalitarianism juxtaposed to the use of power differentials, that portray mythical leaders, that delineate personal characteristics and character traits, and that draw comparisons between men and women. Each of these definitions ultimately combines personal characteristics, gender, and contexts that act on issues of instrumentation and drive interpersonal exchanges and productivity. Each of these may have different emphases; for example, a designated character type—say, charismatic—may be described as employing collaborative decision making. In another example, the individual may have been born to lead and thus been able to capitalize on circumstances that engaged his natural talents. The individual in this case is born with abilities, rather than learning them or cultivating and practicing them or acquiring them as a result of exposure to models. These are but a few of the possibilities explaining individuals' demonstrations of their leadership abilities. Notwithstanding the nature of these representations, they offer perspectives that individuals might find helpful and apply to their particular circumstances.

These definitions of leadership and the categories under which they fall have been central to the way leadership has been conceptualized. Although several are recent additions—gender comparison, for example—they have become classic ways of representing the formal leadership role and individuals assuming those roles.

TASK-RELATED DISCUSSIONS OF LEADERSHIP

Such representations are central to "how-to" series on leadership practice, as well as discussions of leadership practices and their influence on organizational culture, leadership and approaches to decision making, and industrial and educational leadership practices. Implicit in these explanations of leadership are issues of construction of organizational culture, the degree of organization members' involvement in decision making, visioning in the design of change, and stabilization and routinization of such organizational processes as decision making and communication. These are among the tasks considered central to leadership.

Because of its prominence as an organizational process, I believe decision making provides a vivid example of classic task-related representations of leadership. Decision making is dynamic. It is a process wherein consolidation or synergistic uses of powers are possibilities, wherein egalitarian uses of power can replace autocratic approaches. And, within the change process, decision making can be a vehicle for contracting or expanding innovation designs and structural parameters. In 1973, Vroom and Jago's decision model for use in leadership training was published. More than a decade later, in 1988, their revised decision model was published. The new model was applied to leadership and participatory management.

The goal in the later publication was to provide leaders with ways of conceptualizing what the authors viewed as participation of organizational members in the defining decisions of that community. Vroom and Jago (1988) take a neutral stance in promoting their model, steering clear of either explicit or implicit values except in defending their design by describing some competing models for participatory management as "touchy feelly." *Management*, in their view, is a responsibility of leadership and a term that refers to one among many roles in which leaders engage or which they delegate.

In *The New Leadership: Managing Participation in Organizations*, Vroom and Jago (1988) offered their view of participatory management. They view the role of leaders as being grounded in a process that essentially involves the degree to which people, with genuine interest, are consulted during the process of decision making. At the heart of their approach is a series of "attributes" that guide the degree of participation, depending on a quality requirement, a commitment requirement, the need for leader information, a clearly defined problem structure, knowledge of the probable commitment of subordinates, the congruence of goals set and organizational goals, the extent of or need for subordinate information, time constraints, geographical dispersion, motivation-time, and motivation-development (p. 141).

Each of the "attributes" involves questions that guide engagement and predict the level of participation, including the following:

> How important is the technical quality of the decision? How important is subordinate commitment to the decision? Do you have sufficient information to make a high-quality decision? Is the problem well structured? If you were to make the decision by yourself, is it reasonably certain that your subordinate would be committed to the decision? Do subordinates share the organizational goals to be attained in solving the problems? (For more details, see Vroom & Jago, 1988, pp. 91–145.)

Vroom and Jago's elaboration of decision paradigms is not always as accessible as it might be, and may at times be somewhat difficult to consolidate for purposes of application. As a process explored in retrospect, we may conclude that our intuitive actions are similar to the theorists' elaboration without the self-conscious focus.

Kouzes and Posner (1996) have been especially responsive to the need for directly applicable task-related discussions of leadership. In their discussion they explore what they refer to as "behavior commitments in personal best leadership cases" (p. 14). Those commitments include:

  a. searching for opportunities, taking risk, and experimenting with the leadership charge,
  b. engaging the organizational community in attainment of a shared vision,
  c. development of the talents of members of the organizational community and sharing power,
  d. modeling and mentoring along the way to organizational achievement and success,
  e. encouraging these commitments in others. (p. 14)

These commitments are expected to improve the success rate of leaders as they draw on their individual talents. This is evident in the definition the theorists assign to leadership. Kouzes and Posner define it as "an observable, learnable set of practices. Leadership is not something mystical and ethereal that cannot be understood by ordinary people. It is a myth that only a lucky few can ever decipher the leadership code" (1996, p. 13).

Other theorists who take this task-related approach in their discussions of leadership include Birnbaum (1992), DuBrin (1995), Jacobson and Conway (1990), Maxcy (1991), Odden (1995), and Yukl (1989). I have not exhausted the list here, as there are regularly new contributions to task-related discussions of leadership for individuals seeking the benefit of this particular perspective. Although the texts may offer more than one perspective, they are listed here for the purpose of suggesting examples of the classic treatment of leadership.

POWER DIFFERENTIALS AND EGALITARIANISM

According to C. Wright Mills:

Power has to do with whatever decisions men make about the arrangements under which they live, and about the events which make up the history of their times. Events that are beyond human decision do happen; social arrangements do change without benefit of explicit decision. But in so far as such decisions are made, the problem of who is involved in making them is the basic problem of power. In so far as they could be made but are not, the problem becomes who fails to make them? (1993, p. 161)

Themes of egalitarianism juxtaposed to the use of power differentials are typically represented in discussions covering empowerment of "others." Transformational leadership is also a focus here. The transformation I am describing refers to changes in fundamental ways of being, such as changes in moral imperatives and social codes governing interaction among members of the organizational community.

These themes were referred to either explicitly or implicitly in the work of the theorists described earlier. For example, in Vroom and Jago's (1988) decision paradigms there are possibilities for leaders to involve members of the organizational community in making choices and mapping out the direction of their work. The extent to which they are engaged has the potential to flatten out the hierarchy or to disperse power more evenly. The possibility of dispersion, however, depends upon the needs of the organization's leader rather than the professional or developmental needs of other members of the community.

Kouzes and Posner (1996) include these themes in their framework. The themes emerge in descriptions of the leader's relationship with others. Leading well and facilitating accomplishment related to organizational goals are interwoven with opportunities for individuals to engage in professional development. Professional development is then related to personal fulfillment and accomplishment. These relationships are illustrated in their elaboration on behavioral commitments.

Motivation for involving others goes beyond tasks or the inclusion of individuals in decision-making processes that are largely instrumental or emphasize production outcomes rather than combining those with personal and interpersonal experiences. Involvement is motivated by issues of personal engagement, the quality of interactions, and the influence of those transactions on the culture of the organizational community. Quality requirements applied in this framework are largely intangible. They are known through their effect on individuals and on organizational culture. This is precisely the effect that Kouzes and Posner are attempting to bring into focus:

For example, one of the quality requirements states that, leaders inspire shared vision. They envision the future, creating an ideal and unique image of what the organization can become. Through their strong appeal and quiet persuasion, leaders enlist others in the dream. They breathe life into visions and get us to see the exciting possibilities. (Kouzes & Posner, 1991, p. 279)

It is not possible to know what an individual experiences internally until she acts upon it, articulates it, and illuminates it with explanations. When these actions take place, an audience becomes privy to such intangibles as beliefs, dreams, or visions. Processes relating the intangibles to others, such as discussion and disclosure, are transactions that are necessary in order for leaders to have an effect on individuals and on organizational culture.

In his discussions on leadership, Bennis (1991) incorporates a combination of frameworks. He looks at qualities and traits. He comes close to mythical representations of leaders, and also perceives leadership as incorporating the instant approach (power differentials and egalitarianism). For example, he describes the influence of leadership on culture. To do so, he brings in themes that are supported in that role. Bennis (1991) writes:

> Leadership can be felt throughout the organization. It gives pace and energy to work and empowers the work force. Empowerment is the collective effect of leadership. In organizations with effective leaders, empowerment is most evident in four themes: a) people feel significant, b) learning and competence matter, c) people are part of a community, d) work is exciting. (pp. 22–23; see also Bennis, 1989)

Egalitarianism in leadership is not necessarily a corollary of empowerment, neither is the absence of power differentials. Rather, the terms represent points along a continuum of participation not unlike those described by the theorists presented earlier.

GREAT MEN AND MYTHICAL LEADERS

Mythical leaders are represented in great-men theories. The obvious assumption here is that good leadership is essentially masculine. To be a good leader one must be male and born to greatness. This also takes into consideration the historical moment, in that greatness is defined by social context. Consequently the great leader must be born at the right moment in history in order for his leadership and greatness to be appreciated. Greatness is defined through a retrospective review of the leader. Moreover, to be posthumously declared great seems to provide the mythical proportion to the individual character. Failings of the deceased are forgiven in the memories of the living.

It is in the memories of the living that the mythology of the leader begins to take shape. And the dead are unable to dispute the grand character and reputation they acquire. Although his explorations of leadership are not likely to be intended as having mythical portions, posthumous greatness seems to break through the boards of Gardner's (1990) platform in his description of some leaders. Abraham Lincoln, Thomas Jefferson, and George Washington are examples of people who have come to represent mythical leadership.

Gardner (1990) comes close to presenting Washington in mythical proportions in the following passage:

> More than most of the great figures in America's early days, George Washington was a natural leader in the popular sense of that phrase—a person whose combination of physical presence, vitality, self-possession and strength led other to turn to him. The challenges that called forth those leadership gifts came at quite separate periods of his life.
>
> In his youth the French and Indian Wars were a vivid reality for Virginians, and the frontier and wilderness were a step away. At the age of 20, Washington became a major in the Virginia militia and led a scouting party into the wilderness. A year or so later he was sent out again, this time in command of two companies. As a result of a victory over the French he was promoted to colonel, and after still another bloody engagement was appointed commander of all the Virginia troops—a considerable achievement for a young man in his mid-twenties.
>
> At age twenty six, Washington began the second phase of his career, devoting fifteen years to the development and expansion of his plantation. But a greater challenge was looming. He was one of the Virginia legislators who met at the Raleigh Tavern in May 1774 and called for a Continental Congress, and he was one of the delegates when the Congress met in September. (p. 40)

The point Gardner goes on to make is eclipsed by this description. The point is that context has much to do with the emergence of a leader. Gardner goes on to discuss traits, context, and opportunity as influences that affect the position of leader. However, the stage is set and the impression is that great leaders are born rather than being products of the confluence of professional development and circumstances. This point is also illustrated in Gardner's (1990) example of Harry Truman:

> It is an old story that unexpected demands sometimes reveal unsuspected strengths; but rarely has the story played itself out more dramatically than in the case of Harry S. Truman.
>
> By ordinary measures, he was a success before he became president, rising from a farm background and early failure as a haberdasher to become one of the most respected members of the United States Senate.
>
> [W]hen Roosevelt's death made Truman the nation's chief executive he was, as *The New York Times* later commented, "without experience, without knowledge, without prestige."

In 1952, the final year of his presidency, [he] listened as Winston Churchill recalled their first meeting . . . in 1945: "I must confess sir, I held you in very low regard." (pp. 42–43)

As the new president of the country, Truman was unremarkable when he took office. His greatness has since been assigned to him by historians and political analysts. Gardner (1990) concludes his example of Truman with the following:

> Jean Monnet put his finger on one of Truman's key attributes, "the ability to decide. . . . He never hesitated in the face of great decisions." Those decisions included the use of the atomic bomb on Japan; initiation of a massive airlift to counter the Soviet blockade of West Berlin; the United States' swift intervention following the Communist invasion of South Korea; and the firing of General Douglas MacArthur. . . . If all his moves turned out badly, we would not be praising his decisiveness. (p. 43)

It may be that few theorists offer great-men theories of leadership in actuality. Rather, the individual looking for a way to become a leader seeks models that reflect her own beliefs and that are found in what they believe to be relevant life histories. Real or imagined greatness will do when there is a need to define oneself in ways that are legitimate and perceived by others as appropriate.

The value of a model is assigned through social context. It is not surprising that there are more great men than great women leaders or great leaders of color. The addition of examples from the latter two groups almost always seems to be an afterthought rather than an initial intention.

ATTRIBUTES, PERSONAL CHARACTERISTICS, AND CHARACTER TRAITS

Personal characteristics and character traits are central to discussions of leadership that attribute success—however it is defined—to the identity or personality of the leaders. This moves attempts to understand and brings individual leaders closer to identity development.

In general, discussions of leadership offer some form of trait or attribute theory to suggest ways of being and appropriate use of instrumentation to be used under particular sets of circumstances or contexts. Gardner (1990) offers a list of fourteen attributes that are reminiscent of Kouzes and Posner's quality requirements presented earlier. The distinction is in the supporting discussion. Those attributes are:

1. Physical vitality and stamina
2. Intelligence and judgment in action
3. Willingness to accept responsibility
4. Task competence
5. Understanding followers and their needs
6. Skill in dealing with people
7. The need to achieve
8. The capacity to motivate
9. Courage, resolution, and steadiness
10. The capacity to win and hold trust
11. The capacity to manage, decide, and set priorities
12. Confidence
13. Ascendance, dominance, and assertiveness
14. Adaptability and flexibility of approach (Gardner, 1990, pp. 48–54)

Astin and Leland (1991) provided a similar list of attributes in their study of women in leadership positions.

Regarding traits that support effective leadership, Hunt (1984) summarized such theories as they relate to organizational functioning. Accordingly, there were two forms:

> In the first, there was a focus on those traits which distinguished leaders from nonleaders or followers. This was essentially an application of the so-called great man perspective, which was the first general approach to studying leadership and had received considerable emphasis by those outside the organizational leadership area. The focus was on those characteristics or traits that separated "great leaders" from the masses. (pp. 113–114)

In the second approach, behaviors rather than traits were the focus. The distinctions, although intended to be remarkable, were subtle, as traits gave way to actions or behaviors. Nonetheless, this second approach was viewed as more "viable" (Hunt, 1984, p. 114). The "focus was on behaviors which differentiated successful from less successful leaders in organizations" (p. 114). Hunt provided examples of leaders who demonstrated more considerate behavior and questioned whether they were, as a result, more effective (p. 114).

Maxcy (1991) offered his view on trait theory and leadership as well. His conclusions were much the same as those of Hunt. Ultimately, he argued that the search for leadership behaviors is an attempt to match style with the demands of the position. He began his discussion with the following:

> The results of trait research were mixed. Researchers became disillusioned. First, researchers could not agree on what "trait" signified and in which

category an ability ought to reside. Traits listed under "task-related" and "social characteristics" were often placed under "personality" and vice versa. Second the research seemed to favor technical and administrative skills. It was a question whether there were "traits" in the usual meaning of the word. Some traits were more a matter of leadership "style." (pp. 30–31)

Maxcy pointed out that eventually the research began to focus on leadership behaviors and styles of leading. Styles were then labeled in ways that suggested the extent of the leaders' involvement in the operations of the organization, the use of power, and the extent to which others were empowered. Because of the apparent inconsistencies with which labels were applied and, more importantly, as a result of the disagreements among theorists regarding the use of categorizations, this representation of leadership did not enjoy longstanding popularity. The approach has also occasionally been confused with character traits.

COMPARISONS OF MEN AND WOMEN LEADERS

Approaching leadership by comparing men and women or describing gender differences is a recent development deriving from the increase of women leaders in organizations in the last several decades. Until recently women were not profiled in discussions of leadership, even though they have always served as leaders. The scarcity of women's stories in discussions of leadership probably results from the ways in which their activities are viewed.

In general, the purpose of leadership exposés and the development of related theory has been to provide examples of ways of leading: ways to lead organizational development and change and ways to bring about transformations in personnel (Kotter, 1988). The expectation has been that there are best ways to be a leader and that those can be found in the experiences of actual leaders and in the research of theorists. Moreover, leadership has been contextually defined.

The realities of leadership construction and practice have also been influential in determining who may be considered leaders and who may lead. Western traditions have held that men lead and women administer first to family structure and then to organizational or extrafamilial structures (Ferguson, 1984; Greene, 1988; Jaggar & Rothenberg, 1993; Watkins, 1989; Weisstein, 1994). This arrangement has been reinforced by associating valued masculine attributes, traits, and ways of being with the leadership roles and functions. Conversely, feminine attributes, traits, and ways of being have been associated with ineffective leadership. They have traditionally been treated as adaptive only within a limited range of social structures, those historically assigned as the milieu of women (Collins, 1990; Janeway, 1990; Messinger, 1990).

Gender comparisons have examined women's ways of being as appropriate possibilities for best practice and ways of being a leader. The idea that masculinity is essential to leading is challenged as being part of socially constructed distinctions that value men and women differently and unequally. Weedon (1987) puts this in more startling terms. She argues that "the essential biological nature of women guarantees the inevitability that we should fulfill particular economic and social functions which may not be in our own interest" (p. 130).

Helgesen (1990) argued that women have an advantage in the role of leader. They are especially up to the responsibilities because of their socialization. They regularly engage in ways of being related to tasks and transactions that are more suited to the new corporate cultures. The comparison Helgesen makes is between men and women. She starts with Mintzberg's following findings about men:

1. They work at an unrelenting pace, with no breaks in activities during the day.
2. Their days are characterized by interruptions, discontinuity, and fragmentation.
3. They spare little time for activities not directly related to their work.
4. They exhibit a preference for live action encounters.
5. They maintain a complex network of relationships with people outside their organizations.
6. Immersed in the day-to-day need to keep the company going, they lack time for reflection.
7. They identify themselves with their jobs.
8. They have difficulty sharing information. (Helgesen, 1990, pp. 10–14)

By comparison, women are characterized by the following traits:

1. They work at a steady pace, but with small breaks scheduled in throughout the day.
2. They do not view unscheduled tasks and encounters as interruptions.
3. They make time for activities not directly related to their work.

4. They prefer live action encounters but schedule time to attend to mail.
5. They maintain a complex network of relationships with people outside their organizations.
6. They focus on the ecology of leadership.
7 They see their own identities as complex and multifaceted.
8. They schedule time for sharing information. (pp. 19–28)

The differences can be explained by women's survival needs within organizational cultures that are not always hospitable. Also, women's socialization works in their favor in this case, since leading is an enterprise that necessarily engages people. Their experiences as children, in school, and as parents are described as preparing them for their leadership roles.

Morrison (1992) widened the leadership lens by attempting to bring diverse organizational cultures and populations into focus. In doing so, she broadened issues associated with instrumentation, such as best practices. Astin and Leland (1991) developed case studies of women leaders in their attempt to explore individual experiences of socialization. They described women who were clearly different in their achievements; however, they did not attempt to dichotomize ways of leading along gender lines.

Although the differences in men's and women's orienting experiences or socialization are believed to have an effect, the extent of the effect is not always clear. Additionally, those influences become more complex when they are situated within divergent family, regional, and national cultures (Chodorow, 1989, 1994; Rosaldo, 1993).

Notwithstanding its complexities, socialization and its influence on the construction of self may prove to be a better resource for understanding leadership. If so, prescriptive kinds of advice, popular over the decades, become less useful. And the notion that there are always exceptions to prescriptive leadership is less startling for the novice as she sets goals such as consciousness-raising and self-enlightenment.

AN EMERGING APPROACH TO LEADERSHIP

The use of power differentials, egalitarianism, and task-related elements are central to discussions of leadership. Indeed, it is difficult to imagine a discussion of leadership that does not either explicitly or implicitly get around to addressing them. Consequently, their continued significance seems hardly disputable. Gender comparisons, however, may become less viable—like trait theories and mythical leaders—since explorations of identity development offer more individualized treatment of the experience of leading and construction of oneself as a leader. Although individual identity development as an approach to looking at leadership acknowledges practice and instrumentation as integral to leadership, it moves afield of prescriptions for leading.

Some discussions get closer to identity development than others. Belief in the importance of knowing oneself as one ascends to a leadership position is nearly universal. Few people would argue that individuals who are mired in anxieties regarding basic self-knowledge have the ego strength to sustain themselves in a leadership position. No doubt ascendency itself would be problematic under such circumstances—let alone managing the daily onslaught of pressures. Self-knowledge at the very least supports intuition, which serves as a basis for sound decision making. But to say that one must know oneself is still limiting the ways in which an individual can develop as a leader. This is especially true when the task becomes an exercise in understanding oneself in relation to issues of instrumentation, such as the design and use of power differentials, decision making, managing accountability, designing organizational change, and building and sustaining organizational culture. The self as it becomes known under these circumstances is associated with behaviors and motives; however, there are also complex identity development issues to be addressed.

Notwithstanding those complexities, this discussion is not intended to diminish the importance of mastering the skills involved in each of the different representations of leaders. Individuals may find that even those found in mythical leaders are worthy aspirations. The point remains, however, that mastery of skills is one-dimensional leadership training; aspiring leaders need to cultivate personal growth as part of their adult development in general as well as part of their professional development in particular. In his discussion of careers and professional development, Kegan (1994) draws the distinction between the focus on instrumentation or skill development and the contemplation of the internal individual. Accordingly, he argues:

> If the expectation upon us to be masters of our work (rather than apprentices or imitators) is more a claim on mind than a demand on the acquisition of particular skills, this has important implications for the field of career development, which has been far more attentive to the development of the career than the person having the career. (p. 178)

For Kegan, maturity in one's career is a matter of integrated experiences (the external and the internal). They represent "the maturing individual and the accompanying socially constructed expectations [which] do not merely change but develop or grow" (p. 181). Kegan's poetic positioning of mastery and identity development in the following quote makes the point:

> The call for mastery in one's work is really more like an external analogue to the call for an internal standard or personal vision. It is more like a call to move beyond the epistemological place of identification with the loyalties and values of one's psychological surround than it is a call to move beyond the temporal place of apprentice or subordinate. What allows one to exercise mastery over one's work is not merely time on the job or promotion to increasing responsibilities but the psychological capacity to find (or, really to invent) one's own way of "doing it." "One's own way" will certainly be built out of a history of associations, localities, and identification with previous masters and mentors, but one will have converted these to material and tools that serve one's own way. . . .
>
> We have become "master" when the pattern we are seeking to follow resides inside not outside. And we might not arrive at this "place" in the development of a career . . . at forty, might not even arrive at fifty, in spite of our rank and salary. . . .
>
> Our arrival is not a place on a temporal continuum guaranteed by the passage of time. It is rather a place on an evolutionary continuum made possible by the emergence of a qualitatively new order of consciousness. (1994, pp. 181–182)

Considerations of leadership have been lacking in two ways. They have not focused on the phenomenological aspect, including such developmental experiences as the intrapsychic aspects of the individual's ascendency to a leader position through the construction of a leader persona, and they have not substantively included the experiences of women. The writings on leadership have been and continue to be weighted heavily with issues of instrumentation and with the experiences of men.

In the discussion that follows, instrumentation arises not as essential or central to leadership but rather as one among many considerations that are factored into self-study and adult identity development. And although self-study is emphasized along with the leader's persona, the discussion is not intended to advocate "self-mastery" or "self-perfection" in the sense that Greene (1978) cautions against in the following quote:

> Many have written about the contemporary preoccupation with self-improvement. Not only is there a new involvement with physical improvement . . . there continues to be widespread investment in sensitivity-training, encounters of various kinds, evangelical experiences, the disciplines of mysticism. There is nothing inherently harmful about any of these. Most such undertakings, however, have to do with satisfaction of immediate needs; few rest

upon actual face-to-face communication among distinctive individuals trying to interpret their intersubjective lives. Frequently, they are responses to
discouragement with the social world as it exists. . . . Persons devote themselves to self-mastery, even to a kind of sacrifice. But there appears to be less
and less likelihood of emotional commitment. Absorbed in self-perfecting,
people begin not to care or to prefer not to be fully involved outside their
circles of private space. (pp. 151–152)

To a large extent, this discussion is based on a conceptualization of leadership and the leader persona which proposes that there is a real place for
insights regarding self along with cognitive development associated with
instrumentation and "domain related knowledge" in the realm of the chief
executive (Yekovich, 1993, pp. 146–166).

This conceptualization also argues that various kinds of knowledge—
broadly categorized here as instrumentation and self-knowledge—have an
effect on leadership and in particular on ways of being a leader. Consequently, explorations of leadership and the leader persona reveal complexities that are both overwhelming and useful. They are overwhelming in that
they are life histories that include intrapsychic events which factor prominently in individuals identities. The enormity of the task of self-discovery
cannot be overstated.

The discussion that follows argues that the leader persona can be
as authentic or as unique as each individual's personal histories and
intersubjective experiences. As a constructed feature of identity, the leader
persona reflects self-determination as well as the influence of principles
and values that govern the use of power differentials: resolution of socially constructed roles designating dominance and subservience or
"power over" (Blase & Anderson, 1995).

The discussion also reflects consideration of the pathways of individuals'
intellectual and cultural development, and object relations. These are bal-
anced against needs related to autonomy. It attends to the individuals'
meaning systems that influence conceptualizations and approaches to leading. In summary, it offers the possibilities for proaction in the design of
the leader persona and suggests possibilities for organizational support of
the novice's ascendency to leader positions.

2

A Framework for Analysis of the Leader Persona

"My mother felt that there were only two ways to leave home: you got married or you got thrown out. Going to college was not an acceptable option. . . . If you grow up in an environment where you get no love and no attention, I think that there's a kind of starvation that happens to you. You figure out other avenues where you can get attention and recognition."

—Samillia

Leadership has been described as central to the way an organizational community functions, the way it defines its purpose and achieves its goals. Consequently, it has become the ritual of new and aspiring leaders to seek the wisdom of more experienced veterans who might help them find their way to success. Comparisons of exemplary and inadequate leadership are folded into formulas prescribed to improve the performance of novices. Although the mechanics of leading are significant parts of discussions of leadership, they are not the essence of the individual who leads. They may well be the least important of the factors that converge in the person of a leader.

To address the needs of the novice and in the pursuit of efficacy among veterans, many volumes have been written on the subject of leading and leadership. However, the voices and stories of women and an analytic paradigm for understanding the construction of the leader persona are missing. This discussion fills in some of those missing voices and suggests a developmental framework for considering the leader persona.

As a feature of identity, the leader persona reflects issues of self-determination and the pathways individuals take in their intellectual and cultural development. In addition, the leader persona is guided by individual meaning systems that include conceptualizations of leadership and approaches to leading fashioned out of those conceptualizations.

I base this part of the discussion on case studies of women leaders. I propose here that leaders are not found in formulas. Rather, the leader persona is bound up in an individual's process of becoming. I also propose that to know the ways in which leaders develop, we must know and understand something about the developmental pathways those leaders have traveled. I begin the discussion with a theoretical framework that will help us set aside prescriptions for "good leadership" practice in order to delve into adult identity development to the extent that it can be considered without complicating the discourse. I continue the discussion with biographic sketches of the women featured, focusing on their emergence as leaders.

THE LEADER PERSONA AND INDIVIDUAL IDENTITY

Exploring traditional depictions of leaders, we find vivid and mythical images. Those images become the stuff from which people attempt to construct themselves as leaders. Images that are less embellished and fanciful are more useful for the novice—they are closer to the multiple realities, contexts, and constructions of leaders and leadership.

Leadership personas emerge from our individual psychology and are unique. They are part of our developmental experiences. In the study of leadership, we observe the extension of meaning-making to making sense of continually changing circumstances (social contexts) and to behavior. Consequently, prescriptions for leading are limited. Effective leadership is not as simple as following several rules for getting people to work well together. Rather, it is likely to be as intricate as the meaning systems we spend considerable parts of our conscious and subconscious lives fashioning. Indeed, effective leadership is part of the identity that makes up the individual, and it evolves within developmental processes.

Leadership as part of psychosocial development assumes the changeability of people in response to social context. From this perspective, there can be no claims to an objectivity that is devoid of subjective experiences. Our past, present, and future come together as part of life in organizations. Considering leadership from this perspective changes the nature of our discussion. The emphasis shifts from formulas or prescriptions for leading to the way our development facilitates assumption of the leader role and to self-exploration. Similarly, processes such as problem solving become reasoned rather than formulated.

In the search for a leader we might ask: What knowledge of self does the candidate bring to the position? Is this knowledge sufficient? Can it help realize an organization's potential? Embedded in these questions are issues of mutuality and alignment of interests, beliefs, goals, values, and commitment. The organization wants to have these in common, at least to some extent, with its leader; such an alignment is important because these domains are significant in the life of organizations (if there is lack of alignment, leader and organization members may work at cross-purposes with little understanding of others' actions).

This self-awareness liberates the intellect and brings it closer to the multiple realities of leadership and the many constructions of leading. Exploration of leadership through identity development or identity status offers pieces of life stories that bring an individual to consciousness about her own development. During these explorations, we are able to experience an awakening less grand than those promised by larger-than-life characterizations of leaders.

Leadership and the leader persona reflect aspects of our identity. To put it another way, identity can be defined as who we fundamentally are, including our values, goals, and beliefs. Although these are not the only fundamental parts of our being, they influence the way we conduct ourselves throughout our lives. In the present context, they affect how we conduct ourselves as leaders of institutions. To summarize:

> Identity is the stable, consistent, and reliable sense of who one is and what one stands for in the world. It integrates one's meaning to oneself and one's meaning to others; it provides a match between what one regards as central to oneself and how one is viewed by significant others in one's life. . . . Identity is also a way of preserving the continuity of self, linking the past and the present. . . . In its essence, identity becomes a means by which people organize and understand their experiences and . . . share their meaning systems with others. What we choose to value and deprecate, our system of ethics— these form . . . our sense of identity. (Josselson, 1990, pp. 10–11)

This broad description of psychosocial development, combined with those offered by Marcia, Waterman, Matteson, Archer, and Orlofsky (1993) and Kegan (1982), helps to further explain construction of the leader persona. It also serves as the basis upon which we can build an understanding about why some of us are willing to assume formal or informal leadership roles and others are reluctant to do so.

Josselson's work is based on Marcia's identity status research begun three decades earlier. Similar to Kegan and Marcia, Josselson describes identity formation as a continuous process. The formation of identity takes place throughout one's lifetime. It begins at birth and continues to old age, "when we come to terms with the meaning that self has expressed in the larger scheme of things" (1990, p. 12). Josselson (1990) moves beyond the characterization of women's identity as incidental to men's. Her discussion of identity is also different from those describing sporadic stops and starts to a psychosocial development that is largely completed in adolescence.

Josselson's framework presents identity formation as largely a subconscious process. And, within that framework, social role is one aspect of identity. Josselson argues that identity is a property of the ego that organizes experiences. "It is an amalgam, according to Erikson, of constitutional givens, idiosyncratic libidinal needs, psychological defenses against inner conflict, significant identification with important other, interest, and social roles" (1990, p. 12).

Each individual puts together the many parts that constitute who she is. Parts that are important for one individual may be less so for another. Different weight is given to different factors: "Natural talents, intelligence, social class, physical attractiveness, genetic aspects of temperament, physical limitation, early deprivation, and traumatic experiences all render a unique hue to the identity-formation task" (p. 12). Along with these, individuals with whom one identifies are also factored into the process. For example, there may be some aspect of one's aunt Katherine's personality that in some way left an impression and continues to be influential. That impression, along with other experiences, becomes part of self.

Josselson, like others who explore the construction of self, views development as taking place in stages she borrows from Marcia's identity status framework. One of those stages she describes is "identity foreclosure, where individuals function based on parentally derived expectations or childhood plans and beliefs without subjecting them to question or scrutiny. Their identity formation is premature" (1990, p. 30). These individuals have consolidated who they are without exploring ways of knowing and being apart from those provided by their families.

This status can be represented in a child's modeling of his or her persona based on generational traditions. Of course, the assumption in this example is that the child's life has been prescribed and reinforced within the family culture and structure, without question—or at least no questions that lead to consideration of a different course. The overwhelming belief, in such a case, is that what will be is ordained.

Another stage, "identity achievement," describes "people who have undergone the process of testing options, then committing themselves to ways of being" (p. 30). These individuals have experienced resolutions of identity issues that have not been resolved by the others. This identity status brings to mind individuals described admiringly as pioneers in their families. They have not followed a predestined course. They may be the first in their families to be college-educated. They may be the first to move away from the homestead, or to go into a profession not already represented in their families. They may represent a stark difference between ascribed and achieved status.

"Identity diffusion" is a stage in which individuals are neither in crisis nor committed to a particular way of being. These individuals are seen as "drifting, avoiding the identity-formation task" (p. 30). Individuals in this stage may drift from job to job, may not finish tasks they begin. These become patterned behaviors rather than isolated occurrences. This stage is characterized by Marcia as regressive; it becomes increasingly dysfunctional. The last of Josselson's stages, "moratorium," places the individual in a period of seeking and testing new ways of being. This period is marked by indecision. An individual may move between identity achievement and moratorium and continue to progress in her identity development.

Although these typologies seem to imply static psychological states, such is not the case. An individual does not move into one of these stages and then cease to develop. Rather, there is the possibility for movement to states that are more evolved. Throughout our lives we experience crises that may cause us to return to earlier ways of ordering our world and for a time hold to them rigidly as a way of directing our lives. Through another crisis, we might abandon some of those solutions as the critical event moves us to question in ways we had not at the time we adopted the original solutions. Development through adulthood takes place as movement between ways of being and knowing.

In this and other representations of identity development, Belenky, Clinchy, Goldberger, and Tarule (1986), Gilligan (1982), Irigaray (1985), Josselson (1990), Laidlaw and Malmo (1990), and others acknowledge the fluid, continually evolving nature of identity. The work that happens both consciously and subconsciously transforms us on an "intrapsychic level, involving inner shifts and resynthesis after new material is introduced and integrated" (Laidlaw & Malmo, 1990, p. 5). Gilligan frames her discussion of women's identity development around moral judgments in which relational issues along with the ethics of caring become central. Josselson's own work on women's identity was informed by Gilligan's conceptualizations drawn from studies of moral development (Kohlberg, 1973, in Gilligan, 1982).

Recently, in what seems to be a far-reaching attempt to illuminate the development of women's identity, there has been a convergence of discussions in areas such as other-American (e.g., Hispanic American, Asian American) studies, the arts, literature, literacy, linguistics, philosophy, psychology, and social work that have addressed the way women are socially constructed and psychologically understood. The goal of these explorations has been the liberation of women on a number of different fronts, including liberation in aesthetic expression and liberation from an androcentric teleological understanding of womanliness.

When we consider the developmental psychology of women or ways of thinking about women becoming leaders, a bridge is missing between explanation and proaction. Kegan (1982) offers us neo-Piagetian psychology as a bridge between research and intervention. It joins identity theory with intervention or therapy. Kegan's framework is helpful in this way and also because genderization is not inherent in his approach.

From other psychologies, which he refers to as "existential-phenomenological" and "dynamic personality" psychologies, Kegan derives an approach to the person that attends to the process of development—to the inner experience of development or the life of emotions. For example, he does not confine development to conflicts between aspects of identity limited to id, ego, and superego. Nor does he attribute all our experiences to a self-actualizing tendency. For Kegan, without the crises created by the biological reality that one is woman and not man, identity development is evolutionary in the same way it is for Josselson (1990). Identity emerges out of a rich medium (context) that includes the social and intrapsychic worlds of the meaning-maker.

Both Josselson (1990) and Kegan (1982) use the terms *meaning systems* to refer to the intrapsychic world of the individual and *meaning-making* as the central process in development. Object relations is a primary, intrinsic interest of individuals. "[T]he very essence of ego activity is object relations, and ego activity is presumed to begin immediately at birth" (Kegan, 1982, p. 7). Object relations is the tension that keeps meaning systems engaged. As a result, an individual does not collapse into dysfunctionality when encountering conflicts. We can think of object relations as our need to be individuals and our own person, to be part of other people's lives, and to know the people we encounter in our worlds. Think of the way we assign our friends and colleagues to levels of intimacy in our lives. For example, at a social gathering we decide with whom we will interact and in what ways. We are aided in the process by our meaning systems. During an encounter—based on the information we gather, prior experiences, learning (socialization)—we embrace the stranger or avoid further contact. There are degrees of inclusion we will tolerate with regard to the people we meet; some we bring closer to us than others.

In Kegan's discussion of identity formation, the term *person* refers as much to an activity as it does to an item. The individual is engaged in an ever-progressive intrapsychic motion, giving *self* new meaning. At the heart of Kegan's psychology are constructivism (that persons or systems constitute or construct reality) and developmentalism (that organic systems evolve through eras according to regular principles of stability and change)—two ideas that he argues have significantly influenced intellectual life during this century (Kegan, 1982). At the heart of these, human beings organize meaning. Kegan (1982) suggests:

> Like the idea of construction, the idea of development liberates us from a static view of phenomena. As the idea of construction directs us to the activity that underlies and generates the form of thingness of a phenomenon, so the idea of development directs us to the origins and process by which the form came to be and by which it will pass into a new form. (p. 13)

Kegan (1982) is more concrete in his characterization of identity development. For those who intend to pursue exploration of identity formation and proaction or intervention, he offers a way to do so. Kegan conceptualizes stages that are periods wherein we experience the struggle between being part of and being separate from (object-relatedness). Josselson (1990) refers to these stages in her discussion of impressions and revisions to earlier positions in development. Gilligan (1982) and Belenky and colleagues (1986) do so as well. Individuation takes place, however, in the change between old and new, where there is a synthesis that moves us forward in the process of becoming. An individual is embedded in context, where these tensions are experienced and played out through coming to consciousness. Clinicians recognize this as gaining insights and knowledge of self and other.

Tensions described here are managed through tentative truces. With emergence from embeddedness in one's needs, a truce is struck—every developmental stage rests on an evolutionary truce.

> The truce "sets terms on the fundamental issue as to how differentiated the organism is from its life-surround and how embedded." Accordingly, "we move from over-included, fantasy-embedded impulsive balance to sealed-up self-sufficiency of the imperial balance; from the overdifferentiated imperial balance to overincluded interpersonalism; from interpersonalism to the autonomous, self-regulating institutional balance; from the institutional to a new form of openness in the individual." (Kegan, 1982, p. 108)

The metaphor Kegan (1982) selects to illustrate his psychology is a helix. It represents movement among ways of being and the establishment of temporary balances. "The helix makes clear that there is movement back and forth in our struggle with this lifelong tension; that our balances are slightly imbalanced" (pp. 108–109). The metaphor allows for the inevitable event of tipping over and the growth that takes place during periods of imbalance. It also allows for the sense of vulnerability that accompanies development. Kegan (1982) does not diminish the stages by prioritizing or by genderizing them. Rather, he argues:

Feminist psychologists are now pointing out [that] . . . differentiation (the stereotypically male overemphasis in most human ambivalence) is favored with language of growth and development, while integration (the stereotypically female overemphasis) gets spoken of in terms of dependency and immaturity. A model in pursuit of the psychological meaning and experience of evolution—intrinsically about differentiation and integration—is less easily bent to this prejudice. (pp. 108–109)

The leader persona is a meaning system that resides with and is integrated with as well as integrative of other systems. The leader persona is an aspect of identity that also has as its foreground object-relation concerns. In this respect the individual as leader attempts to balance autonomy or separateness and belonging or community.

Josselson's identity stages are not lost in this neo-Piagetian psychology. Within each stage (foreclosure, diffusion, moratorium, and achievement), the tensions exist and stimulate development. Foreground for these is the same as it is in the helix metaphor: It is the individual's relatedness to her object world (environment). Embeddedness holds a similar meaning, and our needs occupy conscious and subconscious meaning-making processes. Emergence signals the attainment of truce and the construction of meanings that liberate. We have progressed and are ready to move into another period in our lifelong evolution.

A THEORY OF LEADER IDENTITY DEVELOPMENT

Kegan (1982) describes the individual as being embedded in her needs. Josselson (1990) argues that embeddedness provides social and intrapsychic context out of which emerges the individual. Through their exploration of identity formation, the two have arrived close to the same point.

Who we are fundamentally (beliefs, values, commitments) changes during the course of our lifetimes. We are socialized by our families and continue to be influenced by people we meet along our developmental pathway. Our development culminates in our senior years when we have a fully developed, matured philosophy of life that incorporates spiritual ideologies. The discussion will continue to consider identity development; however, it will focus more narrowly on the leader persona as an aspect of identity. It is based on my study of women's construction of their leader personas.

The study took 3 years to complete. During that time, I met with eight women and asked them to talk about themselves as leaders. The course of the discussion ranged from their present construction of their leader persona to family history and the context that background provided in the construction of their leader persona. Through these life sketches, we explored their experiences with their families of origin, schooling (primary, secondary, and college), and career choices. The exploration follows closely what Marcia describes as domains relating to identity status assessment.

Marcia (1993) begins his approach to exploring identity by defining it as a "stage of ego growth" (p. 5). This is consistent with Josselson's definition and similar to Kegan's, although Kegan emphasizes the management of the tension in object relations. Marcia refers to this as a dialectic process ending in synthesis. In addition, there exist systonic and dystonic poles at each developmental stage (drawing on Erikson's psychological growth stages; see Marcia et al., 1993, p. 4).

While Kegan argues in favor of a conscious proactive characterization of identity development, Marcia (1993) puts this proposition in yet more definitive terms. He distinguishes identity formation from the construction of identity. Accordingly, he proposes:

> The formation of an identity is different, however, from the construction of an identity. In experiential terms, one becomes progressively aware of one's basic characteristics and one's position in the world. For example, one comes gradually to realize that one is separate from one's mother, the child of one's own parents, the possessor of specific skills and needs, a pupil in a particular school, a member of certain religious groups, the citizen of a specific country. This list describes a given or conferred identity, of whose elements an individual becomes progressively aware. I contrast, identity begins to be constructed when the individual begins to make decisions about who to be, with which group to affiliate, what beliefs to adopt, what interpersonal values to espouse, and what occupational direction to pursue. Most though not all individuals "have" an identity in the original Eriksonian sense. Only some, however, have a self-constructed identity that is based upon superimposition of decision-making processes on the given or conferred identity. (p. 7)

It is this construction within the domains described earlier—including interests, beliefs, goals, values, and commitments—that Marcia refers to as structural, phenomenological, and behavioral. These will be presented in more detail later in this discussion.

Marcia proposed that the pathway implied in these domains is a significant context for understanding identity status. As a result of her studies of women, Josselson adds relationships to those domains that yield insight into identity development. That relationships are of concern to women, perhaps more so than to men, is proposed by Gilligan (1982) as well.

WOMEN'S CONSTRUCTION OF THEIR LEADER PERSONA

The women who participated in my study were presidents or chief executives of colleges, universities, and state central administrative offices for education at the time of the interviews. The terms of office ranged from recent appointments to careers of more than 10 years. The identity status interviews were unstructured but focused. Time with each of the women was limited. The sketches provided snapshots from the lives of the women and served as points of reference from present to past through the development and emergence of their leader personas.

Discussion sessions were conducted by telephone and in person. For some of the women, sessions took place several times a month during the study, while for others once a month. Still others met with me for single sessions lasting several hours. Time and distance dictated the frequency and duration of the sessions, as well as the fact that the women's schedules were generally quite full. During the sessions the women moved through streams of consciousness stimulated by the questions I posed. I used the questions to direct the sessions, albeit somewhat loosely, while the women roamed the terrain of their thinking about themselves and their role and functioning as leaders. The exploration included antecedent conditions such as,

> relationship with and identification with parents; exposure to parenting styles; adult role models and mentoring; family, school, and peer norms regarding gender and social roles; extent of exposure to identity alternatives; and early childhood identity as foundation. (Waterman, 1993, p. 46)

The sessions were deliberately intrusive. The women were admirably candid. People often tend to be reluctant to talk about themselves unabashedly and to move beyond behavioral descriptions of the way they live and survive in their worlds. The women welcomed gentle probing and the opportunity to spend regularly scheduled periods of time thinking about themselves as leaders and their leadership practices.

The understanding struck with the women involved exploration of their subjective experiences of constructing themselves as leaders. Although they were willing to accommodate my intrusions into their personal lives, this discussion is not intended to provide intimate details of their lives or to reveal and emphasize any inadequacies as individuals or as leaders. Rather, it will move from detailed to more general accounts of the constructions of their leader personas. I use pseudonyms to further shield participants from unnecessary public disclosure. Although the experiences of all the women influence this discussion, three of the women are treated more prominently.

Samillia's Leader Design

Samillia, the youngest of the women interviewed for this study, is in her mid-forties. She is the eldest daughter of four children. Samillia's countenance is inviting. She is at once gracious and friendly. There is an energy that moves with her as she greets people coming into her modestly appointed office. Her charge, Northern College, is located in a quaint, affluent community just outside a large metropolitan area. It is an urban school designed to meet the needs of a diverse urban population. Northern's neighboring schools are among the most popular and renowned institutions in the region. They compete nationally for students.

At the time of the study, Northern was facing difficult times. It needed to bolster its financial base in order to keep up its appearance, compete for students in the area, and survive into the next century. Northern seemed to need the kind of energy and expertise Samillia was hired to bring to it. Indeed, the match between the institution and its new president seemed to be excellent.

Samillia completed her undergraduate studies with a degree from Southwestern State University. Prior to Southwestern, she had attended a New York school. She described the change in educational environments as "the worst culture shock in the world." She finished her first year of college with a C average and "decided marriage was a better option than continuing." Samillia's husband was a matriculating student as well. She followed him to medical school. At Southwestern Samillia earned a master's degree, and went on to earn a doctorate from Middlesex University. Between college and graduate school, Samillia found herself alone raising her child.

Samillia began working as a community organizer advocating services for African Americans and Hispanics. She taught in public schools and then became a supervisor of bilingual high school programs. At one time she worked as a director of bilingual and international services in the department of postsecondary schools. Samillia worked with faculty and other administrators on campuses to provide direct services to students with limited proficiency in English. After receiving her doctorate, Samillia went to work for a state board of regents. From that position she moved on to a presidency position at a community college and then to become president of Northern.

There seem to be few questions in Samillia's mind as to who she is and how she arrived at Northern College. Samillia traces her development as

a leader through several periods in her life. She begins with the most recent and works backward to her childhood and growing up as the eldest
daughter with responsibility for caring for her two brothers and a younger
sister. Although she had an older brother, as the eldest of the two girls in
her family Samillia was assigned the responsibilities of the elder of the
family children. Samillia is a first-generation immigrant to the United States
from the Caribbean. Shortly after moving his family to the United States,
Samillia's father simply disappeared. To support the family, her mother
went to work in a garment factory. Samillia lived with her mother and siblings in the city. At the age of 10 she could feed what was effectively her
household on $20 a week. Samillia negotiated with vendors and traveled
the streets of the city as a young woman with significant responsibilities.

Samillia has taken the best experiences from the many she has had and
used them to build the individual who is president of Northern College.
She is clear on what she believes were problematic expressions of the place
of women in her family culture and the fact that she had to reject many of
the values she grew up with in order to be a leader. She describes her life
as a woman-child. She perceives her life at that time as unfair, a period
when she found little support from her family to achieve scholastically or
to develop intellectually and socially. Young men or boys in her culture
are permitted to do whatever they want, to explore their world. Young girls,
particularly the eldest, are responsible for caregiving.

While other girls were pretending to be grown-up, Samillia's reality
had designated her as a caregiver, surrogate mother—a burdensome responsibility for a child of the twentieth century. At an early age, Samillia's
relationship to others was defined in conflicting ways. She was a caregiver
and child; her work as a caregiver was consuming. As an adult she briefly
embraced her family values out of fear of the unknown (the culture she
encountered as a freshmen in college). After an attempt to build her own
family based on those values, she rejected dichotomous versions of them
and began to integrate the caregiver role with intellectual and career
achievements. She found support for this change in extrafamilial cultures
and relationships. Samillia's developmental path is implied in the following excerpt from her narrative of her life as a child through her early adult
years and career development:

> It was difficult for me to learn English. I had to come home from
> school and do things; I couldn't play. In school you are restricted,
> and there isn't much time for talking and getting to know people.
> So I couldn't catch on to the language. For my brothers it was very
> easy because they were out playing most of the time. I worked
> harder. It took me a year or two longer to really learn English. I

recall one year—I was determined to try to do well. I brought home my report card and it was pretty good (A's and B's). We lived in an apartment and my grandparents lived right across the hall. My grandfather was the head of the family. We were lined up to present our report cards to him. My brother, who was very bright, was one of those mischievous kids who never did what he was supposed to do. He brought this horrible report card home (F's and maybe one D). My grandfather laughed and said, "He's never going to change." I showed him my report card; he said, "Oh, you got a B— you have to try harder."

Regarding women, his attitude was: You're not going to live up to anything—you're not going to go to school—you are not going to be educated because those options are not available to you. I was so angry at that moment. I did not show him my report card again after that.

In junior high school, I had a science teacher who took an interest in me. I don't know why, but she liked me. She thought I was smart. She nominated me to compete for a chance to go to a science camp. For admission to camp, I took a science exam. It was a citywide exam. I must have done okay because I was selected to go to the camp. Only 20 kids in the city attended the camp. I went upstate for a month. There were different kinds of people at the camp. It was a very different experience. It made me realize that there were people who liked the way I could excel. There were other options, other worlds where women were in charge of some things. It also told me that I could use my brains. I could figure out ways to get away from home. A year after that, I was selected for the early discovery college program.

School was fair because grades were fair, assigned according to how you did on your exams. It had nothing to do with where you were growing up.

My family knew that I wanted to go to school. My mother felt that there were only two ways to leave home: you got married or you got thrown out. Going to college was not an acceptable option. I had to forge her signature on the application.

When it was time for me to leave, I was told to pack up everything and not to come back.

If you grow up in an environment where you get no love and no attention, I think that there's a kind of starvation that happens to you. You figure out other avenues where you can get attention and recognition.

Samillia evolved from child caregiver to caregiving as a parent and as a chief executive who facilitates development of faculty and staff at the institution she leads. She has developed from an individual feeling powerless and uneducated to an educated, independent individual who views her leadership role as one that should empower and help individuals to transform themselves through their accomplishments. Samillia's perception of self is compatible with the requirements of leader as she experiences the role.

As she fulfilled the demands of surrogate parenting, Samillia began to draw distinctions between family values and obligations and obligations and values within public organizations such as school and public service agencies. From these she has shaped her own set of obligations and values. Samillia figured out that she disagreed with the rules for women dictated in her family culture. For her, women ought to be valued as men are and ought to be rewarded for their achievements. Her definition of self moved her beyond the rigid parameters of her earlier life. Samillia's definition has allowed her to recover from the termination of her marriage (a relationship in which she was heavily invested), to parent her child, and to build a successful career as a leader.

Anna's Destiny

Anna is a tall, thin, regal individual who speaks with a strong, steady voice. She does not look away or inward when she speaks. She is aware of and comfortable with her audience. Anna appears always prepared to meet people; there are no signs of hesitation in her approach. At the time of this study, Anna had been president of her institution for more than a decade—a long tenure for a college president, but not rare. Anna received her undergraduate degree from one of the Seven Sister colleges. She earned a master's degree in philosophy and taught philosophy before taking a position as freshman dean and completing her doctorate, also in philosophy. In 1970, Anna became dean of the college. Seven years later she was asked to serve as acting president. In 1978, after reviewing the pool of applicants, the college trustees asked her to take the position of president. Her charge, Eastern College, is considered one of the premier schools in the country. Under her leadership, the school has doubled its endowment and is now financially secure. Its academic departments are thriving centers of intellectual activity.

Anna's ascendancy to president was supported by her colleagues at the same institution that awarded her her doctorate in philosophy. In a real sense, Eastern cultivated its own in the leadership of this president. Anna

was assistant dean and a philosophy professor at the time she was escorted
to a campus function by a colleague who introduced her as the future president of Eastern College. Anna describes herself as not being terribly self-
reflective. When pressed, she recounted some of the experiences that helped
shape her leadership identity, including growing up in a household with
parents who believed in individual responsibility not only for improving
one's own life but for changing the human condition as well. Anna's parents were activists. Her mother, in particular, was a civil rights advocate
and schoolteacher. At one time, Anna had wanted to be a teacher like her
mother. She taught philosophy before going on to pursue a doctorate in
the same field and a career in postsecondary school administration. While
she was still teaching, she led local desegregation attempts.

In addition to the many other ways she reflects her family values in
"taking charge and getting things done rather than simply complaining,"
Anna took on leadership roles as early as fifth grade, when she was president of her class. She continued to hold leadership positions as she got older
and added civil rights advocacy as well. Anna grew up in a family that
enlarged its boundaries—a family where, as a matter of course, life within
included the kinds of relationships described by Kegan as balancing between interpersonal and institutional boundaries.

The following interview excerpt illustrates the compatibility of Anna's
intrafamilial experiences, the individual she has become, and the leadership
positions she has held. It illustrates the profound influence of her intrafamilial
experiences and the way her parents have helped shape her identity:

> I guess I realized fairly early on that most people don't like making
> decisions. Most people don't like to do the hard work.
>
> I took leadership positions all the way through school, all the
> way through college, and I think one of the reasons I did that was
> because I was frustrated with people who don't make decisions. I
> also see how it is that I could get from here to there, and other
> people don't want to put in the time or the effort to do that. I
> enjoyed seeing that, in fact, I could make some things work and I
> could get people organized around trying to achieve something that
> everybody seemed to want to have happen and nobody knew how
> to do—I seemed to know how to do it.
>
> In the end, as it turned out, I kept getting elected to do things
> because I seemed to figure out how to manage them. I didn't find it
> too hard to make decisions. I did think it was kind of a challenge to
> figure out how to get there, how to get people organized and make
> it happen. I'm usually fairly happy in the institutional settings, and
> a lot of people aren't.

I had a mother who was a real take-charge person. She did not have patience with things not getting done. She had a lot of energy. If people were moaning in corners or whining about their situation, she got very impatient. Her response would be: Fix it up—obviously you like it like this because you're not doing something to make it better.

I think my siblings are active people. I don't think any of us are particularly moaners—victimized by society. I think we figure out how to move it along, how to address a situation that seems to us inequitable or unfair.

Mother worked full-time, raised a bunch of kids, and took care of an entire household. She taught English. She always had time for whatever it was that was happening. When I think back on it, we all took her for granted—I don't know how she did anything. If there were things that were not going right, in a school situation, she did something about it. I recall an experience early in my life that really made a difference in my life. She took me into a store to purchase something. At one point, I wandered back to her at the checkout line and when we got out of the store I took out a Chiclet box and very proudly said, "Look what I got." She asked me "Where did you get that?" I said I had picked it up. She stopped right away and she got down on the pavement and she explained why I could not do that. Then she said, "We're going back into the store, you're going to take that to the manager and explain what you did, you're going to apologize, and you are going to pay for it." I was horrified and humiliated. We went back into the store. She told the manager I had something to say; the manager said, "Don't worry about it." My mother said, "Don't do that to her. You sit down and listen to her." The manager had to go through the whole thing and take my money.

My mother was somebody who made things happen. She decided much later that Black children are going to be getting the real short end of the stick. She already had a full-time job teaching, but decided that she would run a special after-school program from a church in the city for children. She extended that program to the summer in our part of the country. She raised the money for her program at a time when nobody thought it would work, nobody thought that the children would get any support.

My father was the same way. My father was very outspoken—he wasn't conservative—but he didn't get into any of the same activities.

He was a take-charge person. He didn't care whether others went with him. My mother always organized everybody else to get it done, was a very take-charge vocal person. My father just went and did it. He got up at 6:00 in the morning and worked until he went to bed.

I think I do a lot of things the way my mother did. I do organize the troops. I certainly have more liberal concerns like my mother had. From my father I got very good work habits. They were both extremely hard-working people. My father had a kind of discipline about getting the work done.

Although Anna emerges as her own person, her development as leader did not require the kind of rejection of her intrafamilial experiences and definition of who she was that Samillia faced. Because of the compatibility found in Anna's case, the more subtle struggles for equilibrium or balance might be overlooked.

For example, Anna at one point had intended to become an English teacher like her mother. However, she decided to study philosophy instead. Similarly, although she admired her mother's ability to lead, to make decisions, and to get things done, her approach reflects a more charismatic style and an ability to gain consensus. In addition, Anna has internalized her father's work habits without seeming to be as single-minded as he. There are more difficult balances that must be struck between Anna the individual and the lifestyle imposed by the presidency. Anna admits that she is more comfortable with institutional arrangements than other people might be. However, that comfort does not preclude her need for a private life, moments when she is able to be apart from a place like Eastern College. The responsibilities of the presidency in a school with longstanding traditions can be intrusive.

Odette's Vital Balance

Odette originally lived in a village that made up one of the corridors to the city. When she was 7, her parents moved her and her sister into the city. Odette grew up in what she described as a three-story corner row house, what might be referred to today as a townhouse. She describes the part of the city where she grew up as beautiful. She lived across from a city park during a period in the city's history when children could play safely. Odette's neighborhood was mixed, with "clusters of ethnic groups." She attended the city's public schools and graduated from high school in 1958.

Odette's father had been trained as a tailor when he came to the United States from Eastern Europe. He was 20 years older than her mother, a second-generation American. Both of Odette's parents worked in her father's business. Although the marriage was not a particularly happy one, Odette's parents stayed together for nearly 25 years. Odette was married by the time her parents divorced and her mother remarried. Her mother's second marriage lasted some 20 years and was a happy one.

As a child and later as a young girl, Odette was interested in the outdoors and athletics. However, she followed the more traditional pursuits of girls and women during the 1950s and 1960s. She took dance lessons, joined the ballet club, and participated in school productions. She worked on the school yearbook and newspaper and was a member of the science club. She and her sister were avid readers. Odette began dating when she was 13 and met her future husband when she was a junior in high school.

Odette had a great deal of difficulty with college academics. She attributed this largely to being unchallenged as a young girl in school: Faculty at the schools she attended seemed willing to accept whatever she presented without criticism, without expecting more from her. She lived with the double standards of the period. She observed young boys and young men being pushed to achieve and excel in academics. She was simply moved from grade to subsequent grade with most of her energy spent in service, holding class officer positions she had not consciously intended to compete for.

Odette describes her earlier postsecondary academic experiences as attempts to avoid problems, to avoid failure by not taking courses that might be problematic. She attributes this approach to having had little or no advice or support as a student. She tracked herself in science, which was difficult for her but less "ambiguous" than liberal arts courses. Odette decided to go on to graduate school. She describes that period in her life as difficult. She faced serious medical problems, had surgery, got divorced, and raised two children on $6,000 a year. Odette thrived academically under those adverse conditions. She completed her studies and became an assistant professor and later an acting dean of the school. Without formal training in academic leadership, Odette had to construct herself as such with minimal external resources. She describes the building blocks for that construction:

> I was always reluctant to run for things. I had a bad experience running for an office in fifth grade. I was always reluctant thereafter to run for things. Occasionally, I wanted something badly and so I would risk an election for it. I remember when I became president of the sorority, the first time it was like nobody wanted it so it was safe to run, but the second time I ran the most popular girl in the sorority decided that she wanted to run—much to my surprise I allowed my name to stay in even though I thought she would win;

it was a very close vote, but I ended up winning. I had the same experience with the yearbook. I ran for editor of the yearbook and two popular boys also ran. I think they must have split the vote, because I ended up winning that as well. I did not have a strong sense of self or a good self-image when I was in high school. It was a different time for me—it was not a happy time. I did all of these things anyway.

I really was isolated. I did not have a lot of contact with the rest of my family—my parents were both working and my older sister was busy with her own life. I was really on my own.

I did not think [what] I did was outstanding. My progress was not one of seeking accomplishments. Rather, my plan was to avoid making mistakes.

Getting ready to make the decision is the hard part. Once you decide—doing it is kind of easy.

Leadership is traditionally male-oriented. Men go into a job thinking about what they have to do to move to the next job, but women will go into a job thinking about what they have to know to do this job. If they don't feel that they know how to do the job before they start, they won't try it.

I think I had strong role-modeling from media and literature sources. I think I adopted hook, line, and sinker the role of women at the time. There weren't women role models in leadership and in business; there were only male models. So I think I adopted a male model. I think I adopted a male model in business and a female model in interpersonal relationships.

In my personal relationships I am much more traditional. I remember when I was first dating after I divorced—I remember feeling very embarrassed to say that I was an assistant professor. I felt like it was turning men off—intimidating them or something. I used to say something like, "I teach." I would minimize my work so it wouldn't sound like bragging.

I think the male role model is being able to make tough decisions and talk down a table full of people—most of whom are males.

People who are willing to be judged—they have to have confidence, intelligence, a sense of humor—they have to be able to have good communication skills.

I had an interesting talk with the president of a college. He and I agreed that the pieces of our leadership style that make it a successful one are probably similar for a lot of good leaders. They pay attention to details and the big picture. This means they pay attention to the inside of the organization and everything else with which the organization interfaces.

I have met a lot of great people with a lot of potential who clearly aren't going to be leaders. There are obstacles that keep people from actualizing. Leadership is a different package for every person.

Odette's years at home and in school were spent in more traditional women's roles. And, although she admits to having a "tomboy" side, this part of her found little support for expression. Moreover, the term *tomboy* connotes unfeminine and undesirable aggressive behaviors. As a young girl, Odette anticipated a period during her life when she would date and marry. Reinforcements for these kinds of goals, appropriate for girls, were subtle rather than the stark injustices experienced by Samillia.

Odette understood the duality under which she functioned; however, that duality in the treatment of men and women seemed benign and susceptible to anyone who would challenge it. Odette's challenge took the form of mastering the rules governing masculinity rather than rejecting the duality. Consequently, if a woman were to learn the rules related to masculinity, she could do what men do, or achieve what men achieve, or have the kind of power men have. In this way of understanding what men can do and what women can do, gender and sexuality are separate. Moreover, gender differences are rules governing one's behavior according to the environment in which one is situated. At work, Odette follows masculine rules that shape the leader persona; at home, she is mother and partner in a marital relationship.

What seems to be missing from this use of gender identity is the relatively rigid ways in which many social institutions at the time assigned masculinity and femininity. Odette's rationalization avoided the issue of values attached to each. Her focus became the construction of an appropriate social self. Odette's leader persona is built on rules that differentiate masculine and feminine behavior, and at the same time allow her to live with a potential identity crisis.

To be a leader, an individual must perceive what she brings to the role as relevant and functional within the context requiring leadership. An individual cannot perceive who she is as being at odds with that context in ways that are fundamental and irreconcilable. For example, if a woman posits that women cannot and should not lead, leadership may not be part of her repertoire. Leadership is, in essence, not to be "woman" but to be masculine. Consequently, she is not likely to assume the role or to put herself in a position such that others demand that she lead. Odette rationalizes that she has not been proactive in seeking leadership roles.

However, to be capable of assuming leadership, Odette must harbor beliefs that she is capable of leading. The term *harbor* reflects both the conscious and subconscious nature of those beliefs. Her beliefs about what she is capable of doing either consciously or subconsciously must be compatible with contextual requirements. These beliefs or perceptions direct construction of the leadership persona; thus, she is able to function in ways that are appropriate within the context requiring a leader.

Odette's rules govern her relationships with others, particularly where there are cultural provisions for power differentials. The rules are familiar as part of the context in which women were not seen as leaders during their childhood and early adult years: Women were caregivers, men managed and led organizations.

According to Odette, womanliness is more personal because women pay more attention to interpersonal relationships. As a result, women are not able to distance themselves from the tasks they must perform as leaders. Odette the leader was created through meaning systems based on traditional male models of relatedness to others and reinforced through intrafamilial and extrafamilial experiences.

ACHIEVING THE TRUCE

In part, Samillia's creation of her leader persona emerges from her rejection of family values that required women to be self-sacrificing caregivers. As such, women defer to the men in their lives who are the objects of their caregiving and affection. The degree to which the male is central to their identity is not lessened with pregnancy and the birth of children. Rather, girls are socialized into these values and traditions through the strict tutelage of the woman who has become mother-caregiver as well as spouse-caregiver. Samillia's socialization did not support a definition of self that would support a leader persona who could direct men rather than defer to them. Consequently, her ability to do so was in conflict with the socialization that defined her womanliness. This conflict came in part from Samillia's exposure to extrafamilial others, or what Kegan refers to as institutional others.

Relationships with individuals from diverse cultures supported Samillia's separation from family and perceptions of herself as a leader. These extrafamilial relationships developed in changing contexts that approximated leader behaviors and provided continuity in shaping the leader persona. Even though Samillia rejected her family's definition of womanliness, she needed to be close to family members. Extrafamilial relationships and career achievement had a buttressing effect in this case. Consequently, the distinction between self and other within intrafamilial relationships did not lead Samillia to reject family members as objects of affection. Without the kind of identity achievement reached in this case, dissonance would have supported a more diffused period of development.

Anna's leader persona is one that emerges out of her family context rather than in opposition to it. Accordingly, an individual who believed her circumstances could be different was held responsible for changes that would bring her closer to the preferred state. The self-directed approach to constructing meaning and to fashioning solutions to problems was an expectation of Anna's parents. With this approach there was also an obligation to be a socially responsible individual. The leader role did not require reworking frames of reference amounting to reconstructing herself apart from her family. It did not require expanding boundaries that defined self. She grew up understanding that she, like her parents, was capable of leading even in the face of opposition.

This match between intrafamilial and extrafamilial experiences meant that Anna spent much of her energy attending to the responsibilities of the position of president rather than constructing and refining her role in a deliberate way. For Anna, leading did not require explanation or exploration of its constituent parts. Who she is as leader is consistent with the values that are part of her family culture. Anna's parents believed they were responsible for what constituted life within the family and citizenship in a larger social context.

Odette compartmentalizes features of her identity that factor into her ability to lead effectively. She gains competency in applying rules of masculinity that require distancing approaches to object relations. She manages to lead, to make difficult decisions, to accept a course of action set by the university's board of trustees. In her own words, she "does not take things personally." By compartmentalizing her leader role, Odette is able to reduce dissonance created by the tensions between the leader persona and the inhibitive features of her womanliness. Those features were acquired through intrafamilial orienting experiences (socialization) as well as extrafamilial experiences (societal norms). As a child and later as a young woman, Odette's separation or individuation did not require dramatically different constructions of self. However, it required confidence in insights which suggested that she could excel despite the lower expectations others applied in evaluating her abilities. Her higher expectations became "not making mistakes" rather than achieving despite any obstacles placed in the way of her success.

Odette's discussion of her position as leader and the persona she fashioned suggests that she was growing less satisfied with the compartmentalized way she had lived throughout her career. Rather, she seemed to have an increasing need to represent herself in a more integrative way. She resolved that the distinctions between effective and ineffective leaders were not "masculine" and "not masculine," respectively. Moreover, she resolved that there were some values added to the persona when womanliness is expressed. There must be distinctions between traditional constructions of womanliness and those which were contemporary. Ironically, Odette anticipated, as she became more integrative, that new priorities could move her away from her chief executive position toward other career and personal experiences.

Each of the women in this exploration of the leader persona emerged from the experiences she had beginning early in her life. It was not that they each had "the" definitive experience that made them capable of leading. Rather, each had constructed meanings that culminated in highly adaptive approaches to leading and living their lives. However, to say that their approach is what one needs to be a leader is insufficient as an explanation of effective leadership. The balances struck at any developmental point in the lives of individuals are complex. From that complexity emerges an individual capable of leading. By design and through the dialectical struggle that takes shape in changing contextual realities, willingness to lead becomes the sticky stuff that glues the features of the leader persona together.

To know the ways in which leaders develop, one must know and understand something about the developmental path those leaders have traveled. The leader persona is bound up in an individual's process of becoming. That process is adaptation

> not in the sense of "coping" or "adjusting to things as they are," but in the sense of an active process of increasingly organizing the relationship of the self to the environment. . . . [T]he way in which the person is settling the issue of what is "self" and what is "other" essentially defines the underlying logic (or "psychologic") of the person's meanings. (Kegan, 1982, p. 113)

Rather than attempt to lead by prescription or by following mythical models of leadership, successful leadership may be more accurately described as compatibility of meanings and meaning systems between an organization and a leader. Compatibility implies a range of complementary possibilities rather than matching individual and organizational meaning systems. The antecedent conditions noted by Waterman (1993) will be considered more closely, along with proaction in identity construction.

3

The Confluence of Past Experiences and Present Circumstances

"I took leadership positions all the way through school, all the way through college. . . . I was frustrated with people who don't make decisions. . . . I could get people organized around trying to achieve something that everybody seemed to want to have happen. . . . I had a mother who was a real take-charge person. . . . If people were moaning in corners or whining about their situation, she got very impatient. Her response would be: Fix it up . . ."

—Anna

The ego identity framework suggests ways we are experienced by others. As Josselson (1992) explains, the distinctions among the characterizations primarily are in developmental pathways and personality.

For example, people in identity diffusion might be experienced as being confused and perhaps malleable to a fault. As such, we would appear to be continuously defined and reshaped by our present circumstances and the people we interact with. As individuals in a state of foreclosure, we might be experienced as one-dimensional. We might appear to be unimaginative and governed by a strict set of rules that are out of sync with the times, living prescribed lives. As individuals in moratorium, we might be experienced as angst-ridden and preoccupied with the classical dilemma—"to be or not to be?" The more adaptive experience of this status evolves over time. As we mature, this state is less traumatic and serves as a period of immersion during our advance to more highly functional ways of being. The movement for identity achievers, for example, is from achievement to moratorium to achievement.

This part of the discussion summarizes the identity statuses and continues exploring identity development, emphasizing leader identity development pathways. The references here are to psychosocial development. The contexts include family, school, and employment. Family contexts are referred to as interfamilial and early family experiences. Experiences outside of the family are specified and referred to as extrafamilial.

IDENTITY DEVELOPMENT THROUGH MATURATION

The status of identity achievement represents a high level of development. And it presumes that people generally are capable of this kind of development through maturation. The reasoning supporting this assumption is that people are able to become deliberate in the way they develop and in the construction of the individual they aspire to be. As suggested earlier, the building blocks of that construction come from the quarry Waterman (1993) refers to as antecedent conditions or experiences.

There is another assumption that governs this approach to leadership and the leader persona. The term *leader* implies, for most of us, an individual who is likely to be self-defined (or as described thus far—self-constructed). Hence the question central to the study of women's personas is: How do women construct themselves as leaders? Identity construction is the hallmark of identity achievement. Therefore, the women in the study had to have advanced beyond diffusion and foreclosure in order to have actively constructed their leader identity.

The characterizations do not represent intellectual capacity. Rather, in this discussion, they permit placement of leader attributes within an individual's developmental experiences, and they permit consideration of the time and context of acquisition and further cultivation of those attributes.

The developmental status of the women described here is identity achievement, which is defined by the three other statuses. For example, an individual in diffusion is unable to commit herself to a career path. This individual is still in pursuit of a career; she would like to explore opportunities that seem more interesting than what she is currently doing. This desire is not inherently problematic. It becomes so when the individual becomes nomadic, when switching from job to job becomes a way of life. The term *career* does not apply because she does not stay with a position long enough for it to become a fully formed career or a career path.

The achievement status individual selects a career path and follows it through to completion. A switch to another career is an adaptive response rather than an impulsive one resulting from loss of interest in a project that might earlier have been consuming. The analogy of the inattentive individual is not intended to be disparaging. It illustrates the sharp contrast between the two statuses of achievement and diffusion.

The distinctions between the individual who remains in a career path despite her preference for other jobs and the individual who moves between career paths but does not stay long enough to be successful may seem forced. The individual who remains on a career path despite her unhappiness might also be following a scripted path. Consequently, she might fit into the foreclosure characterization as well.

The distinction between diffusion and foreclosure may at times be the more subtle features of a status. As I suggested, the decision to be committed to a course, however unhappy the individual doing so might be, is the glue that sticks the individual to her present circumstances. The prescription in foreclosure is the binding agent. The identity achievement individual has come to her career path through testing emergent philosophical perspectives and through the less heady process of trial-and-error. This individual has processed what she believes about life, her existence, her responsibilities to herself and others, the capabilities of others, and the cost and benefits of a particular lifestyle. The term *processed* denotes the internal assessment as ongoing. It also denotes the dynamics of striking balances or lifestyle compromises.

Ultimately, the identity achievement individual has struck a balance that allows her to be adaptive, highly functional, independent, and self-directed. As a constellation of attributes, these fit the leader persona well. This individual brings the high level of development she has reached to her leadership role. Regarding the tension in object relations and the transition to adaptive, highly functional periods, there was a dynamic that emerged in the case of the women discussed here. In some cases it involved influences from the moral and ethical domains. Those influences included, for example, the use of power differentials, and mediated the behavioral aspects of leadership and interactions with others.

The individual who is immersed in life-path issues is in moratorium, a period of the developmental cycle during which she is reconciling her life experiences. It is useful to distinguish moratorium as a way of being throughout a lifetime from a way of being periodically. It is difficult to conceptualize this particular status as a way of being throughout an entire lifetime. Rather than as a characterization of a phase of identity development, it seems more suited as a transition stage. It is the stage of transition experienced by identity achievers. As well, it is most likely that individuals move between this state and achievement as part of the process of adaptation.

The women of this study moved successfully through life experiences, taking from them insights that seemed to serve them well. Those experiences represented opportunities to explore ways of being, ways of managing, ways of understanding, and ways of constructing meaning as life unfolded.

Balancing the tensions between the private and public individual (socially constructed and normed identity), as well as the tensions with others, is a relevant process in the development and consolidation of the leader persona. Although it is represented as positive, there are changes within identity development that may be regressive. This is a point the identity assessment frameworks make more evident. However, more consistently, regression for identity achievement is to retreat to moratorium, explained earlier as a transition stage.

The tension between being part of and separate from represents the balance of the relationship between the leader and those who are led. The details of this relationship are found in dominant characteristics of individuals who are identity achievers:

1. regulation of self-esteem,
2. the exercise of self-calming function and containment of effective function in response to stress,
3. autonomous organization of motives resources to anticipate and meet adaptive demands. (Marcia, 1993, p. 22)

In their essence these are modes of "control" and "valuation" (Marcia, 1993). The distinction here is between the predominance of externally based versus internally derived meaning systems.

For example, in the identity diffusion state the individual is externally oriented. The individual does not function in the ways implied in the characteristics listed above. To be externally oriented as such is not inherently problematic, and this kind of sensitivity might even be highly valued. An individual managing a reorganization project might be better able to assess the influence of the initiative on the lives of members of the organization, anticipate what could be stressful activities, and facilitate a smoother transition from the old structure to the new. However, to be externally oriented becomes less functional when it is central to one's identity to the exclusion of internally mediating structures.

Those structures are generally taken for granted until the individual finds herself caught up in her own personal transformation or witnesses the struggle of friends, colleagues, loved ones, and even strangers to destabilize and attempt to reestablish the balance, real or imagined, that once existed in their lives.

The women in this discussion are individuals whose identities paralleled identity achievement. The stable, more consolidated structure represents the convergence of "I" from a lifetime of learning, where the individual, as one who began new, has matured. The individual develops from infant, preadolescent child, to adolescent, young adult, and eventually to elder. The individual progresses from one who is new, who seeks to know herself and builds identity. This individual eventually combines knower with known. The sage is also learner. The individual searches for "self" and makes discoveries throughout her life, moving between feeling sure to less sure of the aspects of who she is. These shifts as the individual ages become less disturbing; they are part of the rhythm of life.

With aging comes competence. However, individuals also aspire to gain competency throughout their lives. At some point individuals are no longer the passive recipients of the wisdom of the ages. They no longer indiscriminately accept what others offer as descriptions of themselves. Like artists, people choose the materials that will be part of them. The dialectal process referred to earlier is the mechanism at work here. Building identity results in an understanding of an inner aspect of ourselves (Marcia, 1993). This is a way of knowing and valuing one's self.

The sense of worth—to be of value in one's own psyche—is phenomenological. This can be described another way. It can be understood as the unarticulated experience of constructing meaning which then influences the functioning of individuals. Constructing meaning includes conscious and subconscious processing of information or stimuli. Although it is described as an interpsychic process, it is contained within borders between physical and metaphysical worlds. Meanings constructed in that place are based on what was, what is, and what will be communicated to the individual from multiple and varied media.

The individual who is in a state of diffusion has not committed to a way of being. She has not evolved a system of values. She does not attain the same kind of interpsychic growth and development as an individual who would be a leader. The individual who lives a prescribed or conferred existence may lead if the life defined for her involves leadership.

The presentation of self, or the public persona, completes identity whether we are in diffusion, foreclosure, moratorium, or achievement. We are also known by our behavior, which serves as a basis for others to impute motives to us and to speculate on the state of our psyche. Admittedly, in this and other similar discussions, structural and phenomenological aspects are treated as separate from other areas of identity, but doing so is metaphorically comparable to separating the yolk from the egg. In such a case, there is no longer the possibility for further development because identity and behavior are interdependent; one apart from the other is incomplete and unsustainable.

LEADER PATHWAYS THROUGH PSYCHOSOCIAL DEVELOPMENT

Each of the women in this discussion has followed a pathway through her psychosocial development and, of course, through construction of the leader persona. The pathways for psychosocial development and the leader persona are one and the same. It is useful at times to treat the one as if it were two in order to emphasize those structural, behavioral, and phenomenological features that make up individual identity. In the cases of the women represented here, although the kinds of defining experiences they had may have been similar, the results are unique, since each necessarily differed from the others in personal characteristics.

As the developmental pathways of each of the women are explored, defining features of their leader persona emerge. As with other overarching characteristics of their identity, the leader persona has been built over time. It involves attributes that make it possible for a child to explore her environment, to declare part of it as her acquisition and under her control. Those attributes are reshaped as the child moves into adolescence and acquires skills that the adult recognizes as a culture or as signs of independence along with a quality labeled "initiative." The adolescent, soon to be a young adult, is testing parameters—some longstanding, some newly formed. The individual shaping is a combination of influences that predominate or recede based on the dialectical (developmental) process outlined earlier and described throughout this discussion.

What is it about the identity achievement status that makes it the primary element of the leader persona in general and the women of this study in particular? The answer to this question most likely rests in the extent of the personal development, the integration of experiences within the present and career pathways, the crystallization of moral and ethical beliefs coupled with the maturation of systems associated within each of these, and the minimization of the influence of stress on the ability to be spontaneous, to problem solve, to discern divergent realities from the standpoint of meaning systems that are not the individual's own. There were, of course, a number of divergent realities and meaning systems that could be identified and that influenced the women of this study.

The pathways of each of the women were retraced by beginning at an end point that was a momentary stop in their adult development. From that point, they worked through their lives and speculated on the meaning, significance, and influence of their experiences on their development as leaders.

For example, more can be said about the competent, regal Anna. She did not simply take from her experiences, growing up with her parents and siblings, ways to present herself to the public as a capable individual. To be capable can be a facade that satisfies extrafamilial judgments. "To be capable" as an act beyond stage presence includes behaving meaningfully and spontaneously. It represents the integration of thought and action. The knowledge of cause-and-effect served as motivation for a course.

Anna's experience with her mother in the store helped frame a moral code that she credited with having served her in general and in her role as leader in particular. Anna recounted taking merchandise from a store without paying for it. Because the act took place outside the family context, it was interpreted for her by her mother as being within the realm of larger social obligations. Anna learned from her mother that her relationship to others was governed by honesty, which was part of her family's moral code.

Anna brought the act to her mother for definition. The transaction between the two can be described in the following way: Anna and her mother entered the social context that was the store and the domain of the "other," or the storekeeper. Anna acted within that domain, then sought clarification of her actions from her mother. According to her mother, Anna's actions could be named (stealing) and juxtaposed to a set of family organizing principles that included moral codes. Stealing violated the relationship between the merchant and the customer. The message to Anna was clear: The Chiclets belong to the merchant and you may not have them unless you pay the price the merchant requires to make them yours.

Anna's mother scolded her, creating interpsychic tension. Her mother then provided Anna with a course of action for relieving that tension. Anna's mother ensured her daughter's understanding of the moral code and social context when she demanded that the merchant take her daughter seriously rather than dismiss the incident. Anna was able to experience the release of tension through the resolution orchestrated by her mother. For Anna there was the possibility of retaining a positive sense of self through experiential learning.

In relating the story, Anna commented on the possibility of another lesson had her mother acted differently. For example, Anna might have received corporal punishment while the merchant witnessed her humiliation. Or Anna's mother might have indulgently let her keep the Chiclets. Each of these responses would have produced a different effect and facilitated a different way of knowing what was a moral act and what was not. Each would have provided a basis for moral judgment and a designation of boundaries in the treatment of others. Anna brought this and other experiences to bear on her construction of her leader persona. In her role as a leader this was reflected in her attitude, values, beliefs, and behavior.

In Kegan's exploration of the "self" as evolving throughout one's lifetime, subsequent experiences come into the picture of Anna as leader and as mediating understanding of her persona. Anna credited both of her parents for the combination of characteristics that got her up before dawn to begin her day, that made her sensitive to time and being punctual, that gave the kind of structure to her day as she described it. Anna's leader persona operated out of the confluence of her past experiences and present circumstances. This meeting also gave character to the dynamic balance between stability and instability, being part of and solitude.

THE SIGNIFICANCE OF DEFINING EXPERIENCES ON THE LEADER IDENTITY

From a dialogue turned inward, Samillia created dichotomous worlds for herself. There was her life as a member of her family and there was life outside that household. In each there were rules that governed the nature of interactions, social roles based on gender, as well as rewards and discipline. Samillia organized her life around work. At home she was a caregiver, which she experienced as demanding and unreciprocated. Outside her home she was first a student and eventually a leader in various organizations. Samillia found home unnurturing and unaffirming; school and work she described as fair. By fair, she meant that following the rules netted her rewards as promised. For example, at school she received high marks for hard work and diligence. According to Samillia, she found this kind of reciprocity consistently in her experiences away from home.

She used the metaphor of an individual starving to represent her desire for connectedness, which was met only through relationships outside of her family. Samillia longed for connectedness, for nurturing, and to be affirmed and valued as a capable woman. This personal sense of loss was precipitated by a crisis in her family. Her father abandoned her mother and the children. The family's reaction to the crisis was a sense of loss and fragmentation. Samillia's mother took a full-time job and assigned parental responsibilities to Samillia. Her mother became focused on financially supporting the family. To help stabilize her family, she relied on traditional gendered roles, norms, and values. This meant that Samillia did not experience her mother as a source of support or as someone who would advocate on her behalf or help her negotiate traditional cultural norms. Samillia's life outside her family was simultaneously an act of defiance, separation, and movement toward self-efficacy.

This difficult period in Samillia's life was made even more so because she did not speak English. For a child with many adult responsibilities, having to learn a new language adds substantially to the risk that comes with moving into the world beyond the boundaries of her small apartment in a large city. In the tradition of great novels of American immigrants, Samillia's life in her new home began with hard times.

Samillia's young psyche moved her to places away from home where rules were fair and followed meticulously. The next crisis came with her immersion in college culture. Despite all of the work she had done to prepare for leaving home, Samillia found college overwhelming. Her resolution to this troubling environment was marriage. This was an acceptable course of action for a young woman who wanted to continue to live apart from her family. It also reduced the tension between Samillia and her mother. Leaving home for school was problematic according to her family culture. At the time, marriage was the most acceptable option for a young woman in both the dominant culture and that of her family.

Although Samillia wanted to separate from her family, the outside contacts she had prior to college were not sufficient to buttress her against the initial sense of disorientation that was part of her experience. Nor was the desire for separation sufficient to console her. Samillia was warned of the consequence of leaving home. Accordingly, leaving home was perilous. Samillia lost her family, including her mother—who told her she could not return home and predicted failure as the outcome of the separation.

Samillia's recollection of her mother's warning was painful. Although Samillia experienced this as a rejection, it could have been an attempt by her mother to keep her home, where she would be "safe." Safety in this sense relates to proximity to her family of origin. Her mother would know where she was, how she was doing, and orchestrate her future. Consequently, safety and stability are synonymous. Although her mother may not have been overtly affectionate, she might have perceived herself as fulfilling her obligations to provide a home, nourishment, and an accounting of her children. If this were so, her mother's meaning system associated with parenting and her daughter's—particularly in the areas governing parental obligation—seemed to be divergent. If Samillia's family had been more affluent or at the very least not impoverished, those differences might have seemed to be simply generational. Further, in a more affluent family Samillia might have had time to be a child and her mother might have had more time to interact with and know her. This arrangement might have created different ways for the two to relate to each other.

School, the fair place, did not live up to its past role in Samillia's life. The sanctuary was no longer a sanctuary. Without the contrast between home and school, school became less of a haven. In part, the culture shock could be attributed to the unrestricted nature of the school environment, with numerous social interactions and choices available for a young woman accustomed to many restrictions. Samillia's worlds—although one was somewhat more fair—were constraining. The rules she came to depend on for her sense of rightness in any world were no longer the responsibility of adults to enforce. Instead, the meanings she made had to prevail in college. By comparison, the ethos and ritual related to the adolescent drive toward independence was imprecise and vague. At the time of separation,

Samillia lost both "home" and "success." Marriage represented the possibility of recouping both.

Constraint holds its own rewards in constancy and predictability. Samillia's marriage was an attempt to regain stability. For a while it organized her life around the familiar and the continuation of roles: caregiver and student. This was a highly successful way of being for Samillia—not, however, in the sense in which one understands success as inherently rewarding. Rather, her lifestyle seemed to be a distraction from the persistent issues that she had grown up with. Those issues included the preferential treatment of young men over young girls, the support and nurturing her brother received while she starved for similar treatment, her father's abandonment of the family, and her mother's inability to be supportive in ways that Samillia might discern and find meaningful. The frantic pace characterizing Samillia's life required a high level of competency in getting work done for family and for her instructors.

Between college and graduate school, Samillia became a single parent. Her marriage ended and she was alone raising her child. However, the life she had grown to know as a caregiver began to complement the skills she was developing as a community service provider and organizer, as a midlevel manager and program director, and as a chief executive. During the course of this progression, Samillia found that leadership experiences often involved caregiving and were at times stereotypically maternal enterprises until much later in her career.

For Samillia, maternalism—within the matriarchy that comprised her home life as a child and as an adult single parent—and woman as leader could be reconciled. Samillia came to know herself as a leader. This understanding was situated within a paradox: Men were valued, indulged, and favored by women; however, women, although subjugated, were put in command of particular domains. Women were not to hinder young boys' development into men. Women were at once to be independent and ruled. As an adult, Samillia found support and affirmation in contemporary members of her family.

The obtuse lessons Samillia learned as a member of her mother's household coupled with explorations of possibilities of ways of being during schooling and employment provided her with the experience and confidence to apply for and track herself in leadership positions. Regarding leadership, Samillia's identity rests on what she believed was a fair response to individual achievement. The generalization of this value required a positive, supportive response to members of the organization she was leading. Although Samillia believed in being directive, she also believed that synergy was possible as she gave up power by empowering others. This was not surprising. Self-efficacy was a central theme in Samillia's construction of identity.

This consideration of Samillia's development as a leader is only a be-ginning, as are the discussions of the rest of the women. These snapshots do not constitute a complete account of her investment both consciously and subconsciously in constructing her identity. There were layers of issues, events, and processes from childhood and continuing throughout Samillia's adult life that contribute to an understanding of her develop-ment. Recall the example of the language barrier Samillia experienced.

Briefly, Samillia was a first-generation immigrant to this country. English was her second language. The experience of constructing mean-ing in one language and then translating to another influenced the way she approached social interactions. The significance of that process was illus-trated in Samillia's report of feeling isolated from other children and adults as a result of that early language barrier. There were also cultural differ-ences that had to be understood and negotiated. This was evident in part in the traditional responsibilities Samillia was assigned as the eldest girl child. She had an older brother who was not assigned responsibilities for his siblings. One could and ought to end up with many more questions about the influence of Samillia's experiences on the way she constructed herself as a leader. Moreover, what is concluded about the nature of her leader persona must also be applied to other areas of her life as well.

The individual experiences of the women provided additional ex-amples of the "what if" scenario constructed from Anna's narrative. With-out that scenario, Anna's life serves as a striking contrast to Samillia's. Anna's developmental path does not seem to be one of interpsychic high drama and intersubjective conflict. Although her development appears to have been literally straightforward and unencumbered by the press for resolutions to issues of self-worth and self-efficacy, Anna did not come into full being at birth. However, she was born to parents who seemed to an-ticipate and facilitate the accomplishments of their independent and self-sufficient daughter. Anna's ascendency to leadership was ideological and intrepid. She was moved to action by social causes, to leadership by her sense of competency, and always toward being what she wanted to be.

In contrast to Samillia, Anna was born into an affluent family. She lived a comfortable life. She had what she needed. She did not go to bed hungry or wanting for the comfort of a friendly, nurturing home or a culture that would encourage accomplishment and assertive behavior in little girls. As a child she was free to concern herself with things that interest children. Also, as a child in this family, there were lessons to be taught by parents and lessons to be learned through experimentation.

Anna was clear on the importance of the parenting she had received and the role models she found in both of her parents. She described her exploration of those models. She compared her mother's way of being in the world with her father's. In that comparison, there seems to be an appreciation of her mother's forcefulness and the extent to which she was able to manage a career, raise her children, and be an active force in her community and in her profession.

It is worth noting that, as she described her mother's ideology on the obligation to act on one's own behalf and on behalf of a larger public, Anna neither genderized nor politicized her mother's actions. Anna gave the impression in her description that it was not her mother as woman who acted as an activist (nor did she problematize her mother's characteristics). Rather, it was her mother the individualist who acted in ways that were entirely acceptable. The description Anna provided attributed heroic proportion to her mother the individual. Her discussion gave an impression of a family culture that encouraged idealization without reverence, without making beliefs or individuals sacred. In this family, children were encouraged to explore and question meaning systems. However conducive her environment was to the task of becoming, Anna ultimately had to be responsible for the work of her psyche. And there were experiences along her path to which she assigned special significance.

Anna at one time considered teaching, like her mother. Instead, she moved into postsecondary school administration. She admired her mother's social activism but chose to temper it with her father's discipline. Regarding her father, Anna did not assign gender characteristics to his way of being, much as she declined to do so with her mother. Anna's father was present and played a significant role in her life, but he is less prominent in her narrative. The distinctions Anna offered regarding her parents and their willingness to act on their beliefs suggested her mother and father brought to their relationship what might at times have been divergent ways of achieving similar ends. For Anna, this meant that she was provided variations on a range of possibilities from caring to social action.

It was not surprising to find that as a young girl in grade school Anna began to assume positions involving public service and advocacy. Her parents modeled this kind of leadership and encouraged her to take on those responsibilities. As suggested earlier, there seemed to be an obligatory organizing principle in the family culture. Accordingly, Anna could find reason to do so and possibly even internalized pressure that worked *against* a decision to *decline* such opportunities.

Anna characterized her way of being as simply knowing how to take charge and get things done. Anna's acceptance of leadership, civil action, and the responsibility to organize people, as intuitive actions, represented her acceptance of the beliefs, values, and commitments she grew up with in her family. However, to treat such activities as solely intuitive misrepresents some features of the apparent agreement between Anna's construction of "self" and what was valued by her family. Anna's proactive choices lie not in whether she would serve but in the persona she brought into service. Her choices moved her from conferred to constructed identity.

It is possible for an individual to aspire to lead and yet find herself unable to do so. She may simply not be up to the task. It is also possible to have the potential to lead yet find no opportunity to do so. An individual may not find an opportunity that would permit the exercise of that potential in a public domain. With the exception of a brief period as a member of the faculty at another postsecondary school, Anna had been a member of her college community for nearly a quarter of a century. This represented a significant level of commitment to the college and to her role as a leader.

In part, Anna explained her commitment when she said that she had been more comfortable with institutional arrangements than other people might be. Anna's world, like her family's, had boundaries that extended into public places. In those places she found opportunities to live as she had been taught—independently and responsibly. The extended boundaries permitted consolidation of position, community, ideology, as well as commitment to ways of being as a leader and social activist.

It is not possible to say that Anna was so completely prepared by the models found in her parents that she achieved a perfect balance in all the ways Kegan suggests are possible. It is also not possible to argue that she stayed constantly within identity achievement. This would mean that Anna moved through life untouched by it and untransformed in any way by her experiences. Rather, Anna found that life issues did not destabilize her. Her actions were grounded in her organizing principles: One lives in the world, one is responsible to others as well as to self, one works diligently to be good at what one does and to be decisive. As one might suspect, Anna's transformations were likely to be subtle, without grand pronouncement.

Anna does not seem to be sentimental or predisposed to linger over regrets, although one might suspect she has some regrets because they are part of the human condition. In her narrative, Anna described herself as "not terribly reflective." From all accounts of her life, the statement must be taken as an example of that predisposition. The connection between private and public context were well integrated for Anna. If she were Catholic, Anna might have become a member of a religious order whose vows included public service. The religious community represents object relations similar to the institutional arrangement familiar to Anna.

Odette's developmental experiences lie somewhere on a continuum between Anna's seemingly orderly progression—characterized by the absence of the kind of crises that would bring her to a decision to reject her family values and background—and Samillia's series of crises and rejection of her family's values. Each of these women offered examples of the experiences in their lives that brought them to their roles as leaders. However, like Samillia, early in her life and primarily around the time of her early education Odette found that her interests were vastly different from those prescribed for her by some of the significant adults in her life.

For Samillia, those adults were family members; for Odette, they were teachers (she was silent on the influence of her parents on her schooling around this time). Odette did not state or imply that her parents expected her to follow a traditional path defined through family traditions. This was also the case, as mentioned above, for Anna. These two women did not offer family or personal crises as benchmarks. However, in her description of life at home, Odette raised significant issues related to her definition of "self." Odette described herself as being lonely during her childhood. Her mother worked with her father, who was a tailor and owned a dry-cleaning business. As a result, Odette's mother was largely unavailable to spend time with her.

Odette had an older sister who spent very little time with her. She was doing everything before Odette and not sharing her particular insights on life with her younger sister. Odette's interests were not those traditionally accepted for young girls. Schooling was traditional; students were tracked according to their gender. Although this kind of tracking tends to be minimized by adults considering them retrospectively, they played a significant role in the lives of both young girls and boys at the time. For example, Odette was athletic and preferred science and mathematics to secretarial and home economics courses. Her preferences were considered an aberration. She learned to be ashamed of her desire to be engaged in disciplines that were not traditional for girls or women.

Odette's narrative described a lonely child caught up in her own thoughts. She was, perhaps, a child with many questions regarding the world beyond the one she was constructing in her own mind as well as her role and responsibilities in it. Anna was able to test out the sense she was making of the world with her mother. The example of her test of moral rules governing things not assigned to her—ownership in the material world of others—drew an immediate response from her mother, who seemed to be able to juggle so many responsibilities. It is likely that Odette's family's beliefs about such things were stated or implied.

Discussion of family beliefs might have been a source of comfort for Odette by facilitating her exploration of the applications and boundaries of those beliefs. Odette's description of the way she experienced her life at the time suggests a social and emotional distance that she, as a child, could not traverse. Nor were her parents cognizant of the expanse that separated them from their child. There was in Odette's experience at home a classic generational dilemma, with her parents working long hours to achieve a higher standard of living for themselves and their children. However, their work and the standard they struggled to achieve was consuming.

Odette was a withdrawn child at home. Her parents were probably able to rationalize her demeanor as retiring but not unhappy. She might have simply appeared to be a "good girl," a child they did not have to worry much about. She did not appear to be a child longing for companionship as she recalled. According to Odette, her parents were not happily married. As a result, perhaps neither of them had the emotional reserve or resources to address her needs. It might well have been that her mother and father felt the same distance from each other that Odette felt from her family. It is not unusual for children to express the discordant emotional states of other family members.

Odette said that she wanted very much to date when she reached adolescence. In addition to being the typical coming-of-age desire to do the things that other adolescents do, this was also a way to search and hopefully find companionship. The prospect of dating offered an opportunity to find a soulmate, someone to be with. In marriage, Odette might have found a place where she belonged. With the distance that existed between her and her family, the emergent individual who enjoyed the activities that typically engaged young boys was not encouraged to pursue her interests. Eventually Odette looked elsewhere for lessons on a young girl's way of being in the world. Odette's role models became characters created for entertainment. She drew on the media for lessons on being a young girl.

Odette grew up on the media of the 1950s and 1960s. For the way girls were to be, she might have drawn on characters such as Betty in the popular situation comedy "Father Knows Best"; the adolescent daughter of "The Donna Reed Show"; the kooky, red-haired wife in "I Love Lucy"; any of the teenagers on "The Mickey Mouse Show"; June Cleaver on "Leave It to Beaver"; or a host of "wacky" women in other TV shows and films. According to Odette, the lesson to be learned about women at the time was that men did not like them if they were smart.

Odette followed the lead of her models. Those models provided the same rules governing gender-role distinctions that her peers followed. She did the things that young girls did during that period rather than pursue her interest in sports and outdoor activities. As a result, she could list a number of accomplishments that matched the acceptable role of women, including some gendered leadership responsibilities. Odette's early accomplishments grew out of her attempts not to make mistakes. The desire not to make mistakes was also related to the desire not to be a fraud (an imposter or incapable of achievements valued within a larger social context).

In the leadership roles she took on, Odette discovered new possibilities for herself. However, for ways to lead, Odette drew upon the men she saw leading. In those models she found confidence. This bias also reflected the period. Rather than develop her role apart from men's ways of leading, Odette did what young girls and women were encouraged to do if they were to take on the traditional male role of leader. Emulating men, she had to be careful that her feminine predisposition did not surface in ways she believed were inappropriate.

Although Odette perceived herself as acting in masculine ways as a leader, during the study the impression cast was more that of an understated womanliness—this cast upon gendered waters where womanliness was distinguished from feminism. Consequently, the term *feminism* was situated in the period from its beginning through the middle of the twentieth century. Feminism represented values assigned in a dominant patriarchal culture. Masculine traits as defined at the time were highly valued, while feminine traits were enjoyed but not taken seriously and ultimately not valued.

To be feminine was to be childlike. To be a woman was to press the issue of competence, valuation, and equity. For those who might have been sensitive to Odette's attempt to construct herself in a socially acceptable way, she was pioneering the cause of equity for women. She intended to be nonthreatening to anyone who might object to what they saw or experienced in their encounters with her. Through her construction of her identity, Odette found ways to be a leader.

Odette eventually married her high school sweetheart, but the relationship did not work out. With the end of the marriage, she was a single parent and pursuing a graduate degree. She continued in an area of science, enjoying its clearly defined parameters and rules. Odette found security in what she experienced as concrete expressions of science. Odette's parents divorced while she was in graduate school. Her mother remarried, and Odette established what she described as a close and mutually supportive relationship with her stepfather.

The gendered role distinctions continued to be a consideration in Odette's construction of "self." This was probably because she continued to take leadership positions and to refine her conceptualization of the influence of the distinctions. At the time of the study, Odette was managing a balance between her beliefs about gender roles and her individual and institutional relationships. She seemed to be steering clear of questioning social values or comparing them to her own. Managing these tensions was not without a price.

Odette wanted a more integrated way of being. She was not concerned with issues of dominance wherein traditionally she would be subjugated. She was considering her life choices in view of her beliefs about the reasonableness of gender-based social policy and traditions. Odette included in her self-study the juxtaposition of those policies and traditions with her own beliefs and values, particularly those serving as the basis of her more central or influential organizing principles. Eventually, Odette decided to give up her leader role, to return to teaching, and redirect her energies toward her family and personal relationships. In doing this she seemed to be focused on alternatives to subjugation, those in the form of interfamilial partnerships.

INDIVIDUALS AND LEADERS AS SOCIALLY CONSTRUCTED

Whether socialization is taking place within or outside the family unit, it is based on organizing principles (beliefs, ideology, values). To say that socialization and principles exert significant influence is an understatement. However, although the influence is substantial, it is not deterministic. The principles may be the basis for pronouncements of identity and what an individual stands for, but they are subject to testing against those being constructed and those encountered in the world.

Samillia's and Anna's descriptions of their early socialization placed their parents within the process. Samillia's mother assigned her the responsibility of surrogate parent. As a result, she was responsible for a household at an exceptionally young age. Samillia's intuitive sense of fairness, in the face of a culture into which her family sought to socialize her, led her to places outside her home to find ways of being. Yet although the support she found in those places was affirming, at one point she returned to her family traditions. Anna found a sense of agency through her relationships with her parents and siblings. She was empowered, by her understanding of what was right and decent, to take social action.

As a young adult, Anna led a desegregation effort in a small southern town, paying little attention to the possibility that she might have been in danger by taking the unpopular action. To her, her responsibility was clear; if she did not believe in segregation or the subjugation of any individual, she had to act. Her beliefs, morality, ideology, and commitment to living in the world on her own terms required her to act.

Odette described her parents as preoccupied with other issues as she was growing up. Initially one might argue that her parents were not influential in her development as a young woman and in the development of her leader persona. However, to the extent that their attention was diverted from their daughter, they were, in fact, influential. In what seemed to be their absence from her life, Odette turned to other sources for direction toward adulthood. She began to construct herself as an adult according to the popular culture of the time.

Each of these women might argue, "all that I am today preceded this moment and what I will become I am still constructing." Along developmental pathways there are moments of insight when the individual knows something about who she is, how she came to be, and what she aspires to be. There is something in addition to this insight in the process of coming to consciousness, however. There is not only understanding of the relevance of past experiences; there is an anticipated influence one might have on one's own future. This is more than extrapolation from the past and projection into the future. It is knowing what one wants or expects to achieve in the future.

Anna and Odette tended to minimize their experiences of coming to consciousness. Anna attributes her achievements to simply being good at getting people to take action and organizing them to do so. Similarly, there is a sense of modesty in the description Odette gives of herself as someone who was trying to stay out of difficulty. Samillia's development can be characterized as that of an individual struggling to know herself in a more concrete way and to develop the skills she needed to be a highly competent individual.

It is difficult to argue that particular kinds of experiences or antecedent events are essential to the development of the leader persona. The predisposition, it seems, is to "be" in ways that are compatible with the task of leading. For example, whether a particular parenting style predisposes an individual to be a leader is unclear. There is, however, convincing evidence that antecedent events serve as foundational experiences supporting movement through developmental pathways.

As a child, Anna lived in a culture that clearly delineated the responsibilities of family members not only within the family but also to communities beyond its parameters. In this way, the family extended its boundaries and its spheres of influence. The family ethos, traditions, and values served Anna along her developmental path. In many respects, Anna's path might seem to be ideal in preparing an individual to be a leader. Recall that Anna learned that to complain about conditions or circumstances carried with it the responsibility to design solutions or at the very least to be a participant in the problem-solving process.

Her parents were unambiguous, supportive, and themselves models of their positions. If a particular set of antecedent events are preferable to others, then it is not possible to explain Samillia's or Odette's ascension to leadership positions. They each had very different experiences. They also can be described as coming to consciousness regarding their lives during their early working careers. Samillia completed her graduate studies and wrote her dissertation under difficult circumstances, including single parenting. She described an experience during which she became certain that she was capable of being a leader. Odette expressed a similar sense of her capabilities at approximately the same point in her career development. She then took a position as a dean.

It seems to be possible for the most aversive developmental experience to support identity achievement and the development of the leader persona. This is no revelation, but it is useful to see that many roads lead to identity achievement as a beginning place for understanding the way women construct themselves as leaders. Consequently, the constellation of psychological processes that go into meaning-making and becoming are significant. The social contexts for each of these women provide a compelling backdrop for this consideration.

The early contextual elements of the women's developmental experiences are worth a closer look. The women discussed thus far are approximately a decade apart in their development. For example, Anna is the eldest of the three. The early period of her development can be located between 1940 and 1950. It was during this period that she would have had the experience with her mother in the store. One of the women presented later in this discussion has this developmental period in common with Anna. Samillia, the youngest women in the study, would have struggled to find affirmation of what she believed she could be during the period from 1960 to 1970. Odette would have been a child raising herself during the period from 1950 to 1960. Three women in the subsequent discussion share this period in common with her.

Social contexts are the forum in which the confluence of past and present circumstances takes shape. Also, within those forums, individuals and family are socialized within the larger culture of which they are part. The norms that guide parental responsibilities, spousal relationships, and children's expectations of parents are dictated by that larger dominant culture. These influences have been referred to as organizing principles for meaning systems. Consequently, meaning systems are both influenced by and located in culture.

Samillia presented the most vivid example of the conflict between what she valued and what her family valued. Her parents were new immigrants to the United States. Odette grew up with parents who were immigrants as well. However, the conflict was not as dramatic, largely because she did not understand it as such as a child.

The context as particular to a historical moment is highly relevant here. The metaphor of the individual looking at sequential reflections of herself in a mirror is a way of understanding the historical moment. Each reflection is situated within an influential environment or context. This can also be explained in terms of "nesting." The individuals constructed meaning within, and influenced by, family, neighborhood, peers, schooling, region, state, and the larger culture of the country.

Loyalty as well as local and national responsibilities were prominent themes throughout Anna's childhood. In addition, there was the belief that an individual could make a difference, could lead, could solve monumental problems and thus substantially and in moral as well as material ways be of influence. There was also a theme of personal ability and the potential to be of service to the country through individual action. The Allies were perceived as heroic in World War II, and the United States in particular was treated as the hero, the liberator.

The themes of equality, justice, and liberation were uppermost in the minds of Americans when they returned home to their own imperfect circumstances (apartheid continued even after its designers liberated Jewish death camps). What dissonance this irony must have created for those who came to consciousness through this juxtapositioning. Particularly for men and women returning to displace the work force that had taken their places when they were serving the cause of freedom and enterprise. Anna and other children, adolescents, and young adults caught on this cusp would find, in the future, that the civil rights movement and its issues could be their battleground, their opportunity to liberate and to be liberated. Also being questioned were women's roles in the social order and what else they could become besides wives and mothers. The immediate distraction for the country would again become war—the Korean conflict. However, the national drama it seems had enough momentum to continue, particularly with the support of individuals who were able to represent the intrapsychic resolutions that were taking place.

Social context for Odette included the media's substantial influence on the lives of children and adults at the time. Television created new worlds and different experiences for people who had them. With world conflicts settled for the time being, men could return to work in factories and women could return to being homemakers. The context that influenced Odette's development overlapped somewhat with that which influenced Anna's. The domestic roles of women were prominent. However, there was also a social movement developing that counterbalanced the role of women as domestics. Women's roles were reconstructed with options for ways of being. This was a difficult time for a young girl to raise herself or to be raised by the media.

Samillia's early context would have included women's indignation regarding their domestic roles. She would also have experienced women who were beginning to come into their own as professionals. Those women would have been hopeful regarding their future possibilities. They did not, at the time, reach the limits of their opportunities. They were fashioning themselves as leaders according to masculine codes.

4

Transcendent Themes and the Leader Persona

"I was always reluctant to run for things. . . . I ran for editor of the yearbook and two popular boys also ran. I think they must have split the vote, because I ended up winning that as well. I did not have a strong sense of self or a good self-image when I was in high school. . . . I really was isolated. . . . I did not think [what] I did was outstanding. My progress was not one of seeking accomplishments. Rather, my plan was to avoid making mistakes."

—Odette

The women of this study are best characterized as being at the level of identity achievement. At this level of identity development, the individual is director of the dialectical process of becoming. This status is evident in the women's transactions within their families with parents, siblings, and other relatives as well as those outside their families with mentors, colleagues, and longstanding friends. These contexts represent the confluence of meaning systems described in each case. For example, Samillia tested her family culture, including the gendered role responsibilities and the consequences of abandoning that lifestyle, against the meaning systems she encountered in schools, in her employment experiences, and elsewhere. Through that process she discovered other ways of being that were more acceptable to her and compatible with the leadership responsibilities she later assumed.

Forward movement along the developmental pathway is generally thought of as maturation, which is not a static position along this continuum. Transitional phases, between what were described earlier as periods of moratorium and achievement, continue. Throughout maturation, the focus of commitments made to ways of being shifts from acquisition to satisfaction (self-efficacy) and a clearer understanding of what it takes to be fulfilled as an older adult. This is, in effect, coming to consciousness as well. Recall the distinction between insights and coming to consciousness. Those distinctions are also temporal. Insight, for example, is an understanding of the present and the influence of the past on present behavior. Coming to consciousness anticipates the future in light of those respective temporal considerations. While they are distinct, they are of course related.

Consequently, leadership as an aspect of identity involves a harmonious relationship among the phenomenological, structural, and behavioral parts of "I." In maturation, the individual's response repertoire becomes variable as its base broadens through insights, coming to consciousness, and adaptation to external worlds.

Understanding oneself and what one stands for necessarily requires exploration of both subjective and objective selves. The subjective self has been presented throughout this discussion as individual intrapsychic impressions that influence the individual's encounters within social contexts. The objective self has been described as being partly conferred by parents and other family members and then shaped further by people and experiences outside of this sphere. When we look at these worlds, it is possible to see ourselves as encountering and then being shaped by social context. Popular culture is no less influential than family culture.

Identity as a way of being is brought to bear upon the varied tasks of leading, including building vision, building and translating culture, decision making, role design and assignment, planning, and policy development. These tasks are characteristically transactional kinds of activities that involve the application of persuasion, coercion, negotiation, and power differentials. The objective self, defined by social context and substantiated through interaction, is imputed at times in the absence of actual contact with the individual. To make this later point more simply, even rumor defines the objective self and influences the quality and outcome of initial contact.

In the examples provided by the three women thus far, their pathways for development of their objective and subjective selves are so closely aligned so as to be integrated. This is another way of saying that part, if not all, of an individual's identity is necessarily socially constructed. One might view leader persona and identity as integrated. In the case of Odette, for example, this helps to distinguish the leader persona as a compartmentalized way of functioning according to the demands of her career. For Anna, her leader persona is an integrated part of her identity. For Samillia, reformation of her identity seems so global as to obscure issues of gender, although they precipitated her quest for different ways of being. Samillia's work on an objective self appeared to preempt those issues.

There are five women remaining in this exploration of the leader persona, each of whom was the chief executive of her organization at the time of the interviews. Their contributions here are variable because they provide additional examples of features of developmental pathways.

TRANSCENDENT THEMES

Some of the remaining women share social contexts in common with Anna, Samillia, and Odette. Those contexts will be revisited briefly only insofar as they serve as an explanatory note for the women. These women provide an opportunity to explore themes that emerge and offer slightly differently focused views of the leader identity and issues that are unique to those individuals. That uniqueness distinguishes one developmental experience from another as it serves as a critical juncture in the dialectical experience. That juncture might be thought of as transforming experience. Themes emerge from those and other experiences of the women and are referred to here as transcendent.

A transcendent theme is one that preoccupies the leader persona. They are typically addressed and resolved as an issue. However, they could also become part of a system of organizing principles. Organizing principles serve as foundations upon which the individual can base her obligation to "be" in prescribed ways. Recall, for example, Anna's Chiclets incident—the teaching of her mother and the lessons she learned. In that incident she received her family's rules about honesty, rules that would govern her behavior in the future. Honesty and trust were to be central in her relationships.

Organizing principles differ from transcendent themes in several ways. Organizing principles are conferred, while transcendent themes arise from present context and are the focus of emergent learning. They are also bound up in the tension between the public and private persona or ways of being and instrumentation.

Transcendent themes are integral to the individual's adaptation to her way of being with regard to leadership. Such themes might be related to the performance of leader responsibilities, definitions applied to the position, the use of power differentials, and the alignment of the position as regards other members of the organizational community. They are not deeply embedded in layers of our overall identity. They rise easily to the surface of the persona rather than from the subconscious to consciousness through insights. Transcendent themes differ from organizing principles in source, character, and prominence. They differ from organizing principles in prominence because they tend to be related to professional responsibilities. In character, they are discrete rather than pervasive. Although some are more vivid than others, each of the following women provides examples of the significance of transcendent themes to their leader personas.

Stella

When she joined the study, Stella was a new arrival at her institution. She was of medium height and her dress was stylishly tailored. She was welcoming and fairly at ease throughout the meeting. From her discussion, it was clear that Stella had committed herself to the leadership of a modest institution with a history of providing service to people who might otherwise not be able to attend college. The college needed to be stabilized with sound fiscal management practice. It also needed a capable staff who could chart and then follow a course that would make its programs competitive. Stella was envisioning for the college, along with as many members of its community as she could get to embrace her plan, new curricula, degrees, and a diverse student population.

Stella brought to the college a courageous spirit, a tough countenance, and a capacity to be innovative. She also came to the formerly all-women's college with her husband and children. At the time of my first interview with her, one of the children was at home ill. It was a nurturing Stella who received a call from that child during the meeting. Following her phone conversation and seeming to set her concerns aside for the moment, Stella talked about the call, placing it in perspective along with her roles as partner to her husband and chief executive of the college. Although she had committed herself to leading the college, it was clear that she had committed herself to her family responsibilities as well. She described her husband and children as very supportive of her.

Although she could easily articulate her responsibilities and could see ways to balance parenting and leading, it did not promise to be easy. Both her family and the college very much needed her presence in their lives. Underlying the ease with which she presented her responsibilities, home and the college promised to be dichotomous demands at times. Moreover, as she considered both aloud it was not altogether certain that she was willing to be engaged for a sustained period of time. At the time, she was president, spouse, and mother.

Stella believed she could successfully manage the demands being made of her. She and Odette grew up during the same period. However, unlike Odette, Stella seemed to focus on an integrative leader identity rather than compartmentalizing what she perceived as a way of being a leader and ways of being a partner and parent. Stella understood the divergent path she was taking with the integration of these aspects of her identity. She did not generalize the leader role. This was consistent with her beliefs about the qualities an individual similarly situated might bring to the role.

She set about to develop behavioral approaches that integrated traditional and nontraditional ways of behaving as a leader.

Stella wanted to demonstrate strength without what she believed were genderized ways of being, including distancing or being aloof or uncaring. Stella's description of her approach to leadership involved what seemed to be an exercise in affirming the role. For Stella, it was important to be caring without reducing the confidence of members of the organizational community in its leader. According to Stella:

> I spent a lot of time denying that I have a leadership style that is anything other than the same one that men use. . . . A member of the faculty came to me out of great frustration because she could not get her colleagues to approve a women's studies program. I told her to go to the dean and ask him to use faculty development funds and bring in women researchers to talk about gender and curriculum.
>
> I am playing a very directive role in a sense, and yet I am engaged in a sort of personal interaction that is different. . . . I'll say emotional because . . . [I have a more emotional relationship with people I work with] than male leaders do. I do not with everybody, but I do with a lot of people and certainly do more than my male counterparts in the administration.
>
> There have been times when I have taken a masculine approach to leading. Or perhaps a gender-neutral approach.
>
> However, I am working on making the institution more conscious of itself as an institution for women. . . . I am working on a lot of levels—trying to get people to change their language. I have announced that I wish first-year students would not be called "freshmen." Some people think that I am just silly. Some people really have picked it up, but this kind of change does not happen overnight. . . . I do a lot of maneuvering behind the scenes. Students [are] telling me that they wish the institution would be more sensitive to being a woman's college, so I said to them—I can push from where I am, but you must push from where you are.
>
> It is easy to identify leadership when people have a particular interest. [I] encourage them to pursue it. It is tough to bring out people's leadership. . . . [T]here are always faculty who are not enthusiastic team players. . . . I have at times made flat-out assignments to projects.

Stella's point of reference for what she does as a leader is much the same as Odette's, but without the subscription to men's ways of leading. She remains unsure of any delineation she could come up with other than a transactional approach that seems to be more easily related to women. This approach is difficult to define apart from the behavioral differences attributed to it.

The compromise among her roles seemed to be pervasive throughout Stella's narrative. On its face it appears to be one issue but is in fact made up of a cluster of concerns, any one of which could have become irrelevant under different circumstances or within different contexts. Further, Stella also focuses on the dramatic changes she needs to bring about in order for the college to become and remain competitive.

Jessie

A chief executive of another women's college with much less competition in its region, Jessie appeared to be a confident individual who was accustomed to being cautious when encountering the public. Nevertheless, she was willing to explore the construction of her leader identity with a stranger. She was also well aware of the times she found it difficult to articulate her impressions and insights on her experiences in developing her persona.

Jessie came to her new role after holding a series of administrative positions on the academic side of postsecondary institutions. Before going into administration, she taught; she moved through the faculty ranks to several deanships and then to the position of chief executive. In the following narrative, Jessie described one of her early administrative experiences as a dean:

> The first time that I really had any reason to be intentional about who I was as a leader was with my first administrative job, which was many years ago when I became a graduate dean.
>
> Before that, I had held some leadership roles—I was the chief negotiator for the faculty union; I was the chair of the presidential search committee; I was the chair of the faculty senate—things of that sort. I really didn't think very much about it because they were all kind of temporary roles.
>
> As a dean, I did really think about what I wanted to accomplish—the goals that I had and how I would go about doing them in a way that may not have been a "philosophy of leadership" but certainly was the first step toward that.
>
> I have always thrown myself into my work. There's nothing half-hearted about me.

Jessie described her earlier orientation to work and responsibilities acquired through her early family experiences:

Work began in my thirties—I suppose that's where it happened—
one of the important places of self-identification. [In my culture]
men worked. I was taught that by the male role models in my
family. It was presumed that I would not work. . . . Women just
didn't work in my family.

My first job, of course, was teaching. I taught for 7 or 8 years.
Teaching was more women's work.

A fair amount of guilt was laid on me. I'm not sure that people
thought that way. I had young children. What was I doing—
working? My family was very polite, they would never do anything
more than hint. . . . I just had to do what was important. I was angry
about it, I suppose. My parents were very proud of me always—at
least that's what they said. They always bragged about my accomplishments to other people, but in fact I had the sense that they
really didn't approve. . . . I tried to compartmentalize that rather
than deal with it. I was not sure how to deal with it. As a result, I
was not particularly close to my parents. In some ways we were
close; in others we were not.

Compartmentalizing was not so much a distinction between
home and work. Rather, it was my feelings about the guilt and other
things that I associated with my parents. I also associated those
feelings with other relatives such as my aunts and uncles, not with
my husband and children. I was divorced when I was in my late
twenties and later remarried. My life improved. My husband was
supportive and my children had been all along. My children were
supportive at a very young age. My husband is very much involved
in raising his children. He is not a traditionalist.

Jessie's leader persona shows signs of the influence of the period in
which she grew up. The parameters for women's lives were clear. Her family grounded her in the traditional responsibilities assigned to women. By
contrast, Odette gleaned from her exposure to popular culture what Jessie
understood as the rules her family followed and taught her.

Although she and Odette have much in common regarding their beliefs about their leader personas, Jessie's unique contribution to this
discussion lies in her understanding of the conduct of a leader and the transcendent theme she recalls as guiding her way of being as a leader. Jessie
focused on confidentiality, or the relationship individuals have with others
who might be described as confidants. On a deeper level, this might be
construed as the conflict between being part of and being separate from—
or individuation as an adult developmental issue. However, in this instance

it reflects experiences Jessie has had in defining herself as a leader at specific institutions and under particular circumstances.

Consequently, trust, confidentiality, and relatedness to others are, for Jessie, discrete leadership issues. These are part of her learning as a leader and contextualized in her consciousness within leadership. In the following narrative she looks at her leader persona development in the positions she has held. She also provides a glimpse at the way she reconciled differences between her early family experiences and those she had in larger social worlds:

> At the time I moved into administration, I had remarried and my children, of course, were older and their demands were less. Administration was a more natural form of work for me; that is, I really liked it better than being a full-time faculty member. I really disliked the isolation of scholarship. . . . I never in my scholarly work felt the same kind of commitment and passion that I feel in trying to make an administrative enterprise work, of whatever sort. I had role models in administrative jobs that I didn't have when I was a full-time faculty member. They were the male models of my family; all were in business of one sort or another. I used those models and, really, that's where I learned about things.

Jessie integrated those models into what became her way of being as a leader. She said:

> One big difference that was actually essential is the kind of enterprise that I've been engaged [in]. My career was a very different one than the kind that my role models had. They were all in business. Although higher education has its businesslike side, it is a very different sort of industry with a very different value system. I had to adapt or develop a style that was consistent with the culture of the place of my employment. In addition, being a woman was a powerful part of my career, influencing it in both negative and positive ways. In my present position at a women's college, I am struck by the fact that I have been an honorary man in my leadership roles.

In the next part of her narrative, Jessie described the genderization of her leader persona:

> I was usually the only and the first woman. Here that is not true. . . . In order to be effective—and I guess I would say that I was

really very effective in that male role—I had to learn quickly to be a man. I had to be less open and more careful about what I said. I have never been a particularly emotional person, but I absolutely had to assume an objectivity. I learned that this was the way work was done. Work was an object. I was a successful honorary man.

Jessie believes she was perceived as competent. However, she rationalized the compartmentalization, described earlier, and its eventual resolution in the following way:

I think of myself as a pretty well-integrated whole kind of self so that I don't compartmentalize much—I have this whole now. . . . In the last year and a half [it has been] very different—2 years actually. . . . During my earlier experiences, I had begun to work through many of the conflicts arising out of my family. . . . For example, through successive administrative positions, I gained a degree of confidence and self-awareness. At the same time I came to know my limits. . . . I have a very cheerful nature, which I suppose is a necessary thing to have if you are going to go into administration at all—to get in the door—I think you have to have it, but there is a darker side . . . of human nature that I think also needs to be understood.

Presidents need to be able to come more to terms with their weaknesses as well as their strengths and with the weaknesses of their institutions and have a life that is outside that. . . . I did not have this insight in my first job.

My most difficult position showed me that I am, in fact, dependent on other people—that I, in fact, cannot be a one-person band and that my strengths really are quite dependent upon my ability to show good judgment in hiring subordinates and in gaining support from other people. Moreover, I absolutely cannot do the job alone. That is really a wonderful thing to learn. . . . Absolutely liberating.

Throughout Jessie's narrative it is apparent that she managed to resolve conflicts arising from her way of being in leadership positions by moderating what she was taught by members of her family and what she experienced beyond those parameters. She did describe, as Stella did, a desire to integrate who she was as a woman with a way of leading. Nonetheless, there were hints that the compartmentalization she devised was construed as competent within her organization and by her peers.

Issues of confidants and trusting relationships among the people she works with seemed to persist even though they did not originate at the women's college. Jessie was not quite sure that she needed to be as distant as she had been. The question of whether to be part of or separate from was complicated by what she anticipated would be perceptions of people who were at the time relatively new colleagues. She had been in the presidency for 1 year at the time she entered the study. Jessie seemed to be well grounded in the treatment of people as individuals who were sensitive to and influenced by the ebb and flow of change within their organizations, change for which she was largely responsible.

Isabella

At the time she entered the study, Isabella was heading a state central administrative agency. She came to that position from a community college, where she had served as president. Isabella was the youngest of five daughters. She lived in Cuba, where her father had a medical practice, until she was 21. She attended Catholic schools. At the time of the interview, her parents were deceased and one of her sisters had recently died. Of her remaining sisters, one was a medical doctor, another a lawyer, and another an engineer. She and her siblings had been encouraged to excel in whatever profession they chose by parents who were themselves successful. Isabella's mother had studied voice and been an opera singer before taking on the job of full-time parent. According to Isabella, each of her siblings had achieved substantial success in her field.

Isabella attributed her sense of self, including her ability to achieve, to her early family experience. She argued that it is family "that tells you you will be whatever you want to be yet encourages you onward and puts demands on you." She described her parents as demanding and requiring demonstration of their children's abilities in school. Isabella and her siblings were "expected to be the best they could be."

In 1960 Isabella came to the United States because of the political difficulties in her native country. However, prior to that she had received her undergraduate and graduate degrees and was teaching school. She left her country with her child and her husband, with very little money to get started in a life they hoped would be less dangerous. Eventually, Isabella and her husband divorced, and for a while she was on her own raising her children. Isabella's subsequent remarriage was to a man she described as "extremely supportive." She also credited extended family relationships as giving her the support she needed to acquire and maintain a job at a community college that was enlarging its language program. Her sisters helped her with her children, providing tutoring; her mother-in-law lived with her and helped with the children; aunts and uncles were also available to lend her support when she needed it.

At the time of the interview, Isabella had been leading her organization for 2 years. Still before her was the enormous task of developing and coordinating the responsibilities of the young organization she was heading. Isabella seemed to have no doubts about her ability to do a job that others might have approached with trepidation. For her, it was a matter of course. She was raised on a script, provided by her family, that dictated that she do well in whatever she invested herself and her energies in. This way of knowing oneself is similar to that imparted to Anna by her parents. Although the two women grew up in different parts of the world, they had common developmental experiences. Their parents were well educated and believed their children ought to be as well. They had the luxury of moving beyond the mundane: food on the table, a roof over their children's head, and a basic education to open possibilities for them beyond their present circumstances. The family culture that molded Isabella's identity was one that also proposed that women could be designers of their own futures and part of domains reserved for others.

Again like Anna, Isabella had a sense of her own power. The kinds of instrumentation issues that might have encumbered another individual's ascending to a leader position and that could have become bound up in the construction of the leader persona were not focal points for her. Rather, she was immersed in the concerns of the community in her charge. Isabella's attention was directed outside herself. She was not paying attention to the way colleagues might perceive her or to the use of power differentials to acquire credibility or more influence. At first glance, the questions she seemed to care most about seemed far removed from her identity. She was looking for ways of building community and of empowering people so that those with whom she worked could function as leaders and be competent. For Isabella there seemed to be no dissonance to cope with in her understanding of who she was. Her way of being a leader directed her attention outward toward others. Isabella was not inclined to be self-absorbed in her leader persona. Instead, she paid attention to the responsibilities of the role, and her focus was on the beneficiaries of the work of her organizations:

> There is a winner and a loser and to me the winner and the loser
> is the reason why we are here. I mean, if I'm talking about K
> through 12, about a child that is going through education—that's
> the person who has to be a winner. [If] certain things don't happen, then that person or that child becomes a loser. That's my
> agenda.

It might also be the case that a large part of Isabella's identity is tied up in successful management of institutional arrangements. Within those arrangements, she applies definitions that allow her to take up advocacy as a process she believes is part of leading:

> One of my mentors a long time ago . . . told me when I was struggling, learning how to administer a program in the very early stages, never lose track of your goal. And, if this is your goal, you try all kinds of different approaches to see how you can get it to happen for you. You evaluate as you go along to make sure that your perception of your goals is still correct, but then you keep going at it from all different angles until you are in position to achieve the goal. That is how I look at it.
>
> If I can get the basics, I think I will begin to cause the changes to begin to occur—then I think there is always time to come back and work on the rest.

For Isabella, there was a compatibility between her role as leader according to the way she perceived it in general and the contextual, instrumentation issues associated with leading her organization. Several of her narratives, like the following one, provide examples of this with regard to the use of power and power differentials:

> It seems like yesterday. . . . As a matter of fact, it will be 2 years very soon. . . . So we actually had to put it together from scratch and build it up. Success in doing something like that comes when one of the things a leader does is to very carefully select the people that she works with. You want to find people who are extremely strong because the stronger they are, the stronger a leader can be. I think it is important that everybody complements everybody else in skills and knowledge. So using that as my strategy, I think the office is in place—and a lot has been accomplished.

Isabella went on to suggest a conjoining of family expectations and transcendent themes that influenced her constructed persona. Those themes included trust in herself and her abilities as well as trust in people with whom she must share leader functions. This instrumentation is significant in that it is object relations as part of the leader identity.

Isabella critiqued her own performance as a leader: "I always think that I could have done more and I could have been better. I measure myself against these standards." In the next excerpt, Isabella considered her leader identity through the perceptions of her mentors:

> I think in many ways the people that made an impression on me who were mentors in one way or the other were people who treated leadership in similar ways. They saw value in what I brought to a department, an office, or a discussion, and did not narrow their view as to whether I was female or Hispanic. They assumed I was capable.
>
> My mentors allowed me to demonstrate what I could do. They were willing to let me take risks and follow the path I thought was indicated.

External assessments of her abilities were necessary reflections on her leader persona. In those exchanges there were possibilities for learning and proaction in identity development, particularly as it related to her leader persona.

Trust was among the themes related to instrumentation in the leadership role that commanded Isabella's attention. The issue was similar to Jessie's focus on her relationship with faculty and staff and on the possibilities for sharing confidences with those individuals. Whom to trust and when to trust were implicit in Jessie's theme. To trust and relate to individuals as colleagues who might offer opportunities for collaboration and reflection on practice were the ways in which Isabella framed the theme.

Although the themes are similar and perhaps even comparable, the implications have to do with instrumentation as indicated in the practices of both women. Within that domain there are referential differences. Jessie's preoccupation was with organizational structure, function, growth, and development, including personnel decisions. This was in contrast to Isabella's concern with assignment of leadership functions, the use of power differentials, and personnel competencies rather than their potential for development. Distinctions between the themes can be analogous to background and foreground subjects. In both instances instrumentation is central. Contextual relevance influences the prominence of either one.

Isabella did not tend to search the recesses of her psyche to find out why she had taken the developmental path she did. Nor did she offer complex analyses of her worldview. What she perceived as her developmental potential (supported through her family experiences and socialization) and experiences she had had in school and other contexts appeared to be in harmony. Her self-perceptions (who she believed she was in her social roles) were congruent with perceptions of her potential offered by her parents and reinforced in the larger family context. According to her family, the world, although not benign, was a malleable place in which its members were capable of continued development, wherever they were situated. This approach to building a life was proactive, based on what her family perceived as a high level of competency among its members.

Elizabeth

At the time of the study, Elizabeth had just taken over as chancellor of a large urban university campus that was having financial difficulties. The institution had lost one-third of its operating expenses in consecutive budget cuts. In light of those losses, Elizabeth was trying to determine the structure and direction of the school over the next 5 to 10 years. Some of the issues she faced included whether the school should be primarily an undergraduate campus with limited master's and doctoral options, or become a research institution and more of a university. Although to remain unchanged presented a set of difficulties, it was an attractive option and one many faculty and administrators would have supported. Consequently, it was the option of least resistance. Elizabeth, however, believed the school was at a crossroads, one she wanted to lead it beyond. The changes that were taking place in state governance were filtering down to the campuses and presented opportunities to change, to consolidate a future in postsecondary education for the school.

Elizabeth began implementing the school's 5-year plan, which had been outlined by faculty and staff. The future of the school included three doctoral programs, a research institution on Latino studies, and a capital campaign. The campaign was one of the pivotal features of the planning document and crucial to the future of the planned programs. With the funds obtained through the campaign, those programs were to be put in place. In addition to working aggressively to build a future for the campus, despite the limping budget (the first of the consecutive cuts amounted to $5 million), Elizabeth made some bold changes in staff positions. For example, she hired a woman to fill the position of chief financial officer, a position previously held only by men. At the same time, she eliminated 18 administrative positions.

Elizabeth described her relationship with staff as close and the parameters of their interactions as "very open" with candid exchanges. During those exchanges, she listened and weighed the contributions of her staff. Even though they worked closely as a team, keeping in mind the goals set for the campus, Elizabeth was aware of the tensions that existed among several factions of the organizational structure. For example, there were periods of strain between administrative and academic elements regarding student life on campus. For Elizabeth, these conflicts were inevitable, given the different way each group perceived the responsibilities of the institution. Those ways of perceiving drove expectations and interactions in much the same way individuals' divergent perspectives influence their interactions.

Although Elizabeth saw herself as the individual responsible for making difficult and sometimes final decisions regarding the school's planning and development issues, she also viewed herself as encouraging participation through collaboration. That kind of interaction took shape in her consultative approach to preliminary assessments of the organization's needs. Elizabeth suggested the quality of that kind of interaction in the following comments:

> I like working with people who are quick, who understand the issues, who are willing then to make a recommendation and take responsibility for them. I like working with people who are willing to say, "You know, I don't agree with you, but I understand your reasoning and will support you." I believe one can pretty quickly sense who some of those people can be. I have been fortunate to have very good people here that have been helpful in this change process. . . . One of the tests of leadership is to find those people and work with them.

Elizabeth provided a caveat to her statement on the kinds of interactions she found most helpful as she attempted to steer a new course for her school. She believed working productively with members of her organizational community did not require faculty and staff to give up all sense of autonomy. She anticipated moving to a more decentralized structure once the campus was stable. She included in that decentralization "[moving] back to more autonomy" in campus operations. Guided by her earlier experiences, she anticipated faculty and staff would find it difficult to resume responsibilities for the decentralized tasks.

Even with the resumption of decentralized operations, Elizabeth expected to maintain her collaborative approach to leading. Her decisions did not aim to disenfranchise members of the campus community or, more specifically, to undermine governance of academic structures, curricular issues, and departmental policies. She was resolute as she steered her campus toward its future.

The confidence Elizabeth had in her abilities as a leader grew out of her earlier experiences. The twists and turns of her developmental pathway included at times rethinking her career—allowing her plans to diverge from earlier commitments in order to explore new possibilities. Here she offers some of her impressions in those experiences:

My father was a school principal and a school superintendent, so I saw a lot of things happening in education. I saw him work with the community, with the school board, and saw him try to help kids all along. My mother was a teacher. Although I told them when I was growing up that I would never be a teacher, there were probably subtle influences.

I began studying prelaw, believing I would enter that profession some day.

Elizabeth described those influences as compelling, recounting the times she shared traveling with her parents to professional education meetings. She did not recall her parents pressuring her to enter the field of education. On the contrary, they were supportive of her interests in other areas. She recalled her father "arranging meetings for me with people in the foreign service because I was interested in that at one time. . . . He arranged meetings for me with people in Washington because I thought about government kinds of service." But the desire to pursue education as both an academic and applied discipline grew out of her early family socialization. The world Elizabeth shared with her parents was vividly portrayed in her narrative. As an only child, she enjoyed a lifestyle with her parents that might have been different if she had siblings who would have also required their attention and counsel. As life unfolded for her and her parents, their lives merged. She was both participant and observer within her parents professional domains. Regarding that experience she stated:

I went to a lot of events with them. I saw my father in many of his roles as a leader. . . . I got a lot of exposure to leadership. My dad used to go to superintendents' conferences—I went along. . . . I got a sense of what leaders do with their lives. . . . Leading is a very public thing. You are speaking, you are meeting people, you are making decisions, your life is torn in many directions. My father was always out a lot at night. . . . I think there were probably a lot of things that were getting into me by osmosis or in some way in which I was not even conscious. . . . I mean, I had in my mind that all children lived like this.

For Elizabeth, life at home and, in particular, her father's leader persona were an integrated, seamless whole. There were no transitions immediately evident to a child who saw her father at school, in the community, and at home. All were contexts in which he was a leader. In each he held the formal role. His modeling and influence were further suggested in the following narrative:

My dad would have been known then as a very friendly person. When he walked into a room, he would introduce himself. I am that way. I suspect I am much more like him than I ever thought I would be. I think that he would be very, very proud about that. I picked up some of his mannerisms and style, but I think that's probably less important than watching him and seeing what leaders do.

This exposure was critical to the development of Elizabeth's leader identity. She considers her high school and college years to be the period when her father's example became most evident. Regarding that period she said:

I think if you would look at my high school and college yearbook you would not be surprised because I was president of this or that—leader of this or that. I was on various committees and I was also a straight-A student. I was valedictorian of the high school class. There were actually three of us the year I graduated. Nothing like that happened before. I was president of something called "The Girls Lit Club," which was the thing to be in, an officer of several other kinds of clubs and things like that in high school. In college I was also president of the sorority, president of the freshmen honor sorority, and a straight-A student.

Notwithstanding her parents' influence and particularly her father's, Elizabeth's development had its own twists and turns before she took the position she held at the time she provided her narratives.

In school Elizabeth worked diligently to be a scholastic success. She wanted to be an attorney and knew it would be difficult at best to gain admission to law school. Her plan to become a lawyer did not come to fruition because there were quotas on the admission of women to the schools at the time. Instead, Elizabeth entered a university that offered her a fellowship to study for her doctorate. She eventually received her Ph.D. and briefly taught at a college. At that time, she had an opportunity to go into postsecondary education administration. Between teaching college and accepting the administrative position, she had taught secondary school to support her husband while he finished his doctorate. The couple's plan was that she would support her husband while he finished his studies and then she would complete hers.

The plan worked, but it was 6 years before Elizabeth finally earned her doctorate. By that time she also had a 2-year-old child and was pregnant again. This was a difficult detour on the road to postsecondary school administration. At one point, Elizabeth became a single parent while she continued working on her career. At long last Elizabeth took a position as an associate in higher education evaluating public and private colleges. From that job she went on to several successive positions as associate provost. She then took the position as president of an eastern urban university. Elizabeth explained her career path:

> The decision that a full-time career was what I wanted to do was probably made early and confirmed in my position as associate provost. I worked all the time! If you are not willing to give that to it, you really shouldn't even think about it. It's very time-consuming. It's very demanding. You don't have a lot of time for hobbies or other things.

Elizabeth believed that there were other significant models of ways to lead and ways of being a leader that she encountered along her developmental path. Among those was the provost at the school where she had held the position of associate provost. This exposure was coupled with her decision to be proactive in the construction of her leader persona. In addition, her thinking about a career, her position as a leader, and how she would define who she was began to consolidate in a psyche made fertile by her early family experiences.

The exposure to the way individuals construct themselves as leaders was critical to Elizabeth's leader identity. It helped to add layers to her persona. The integration of her leader persona with the individual she was, apart from the leadership role, was a noteworthy theme emerging from her narratives. This theme was obvious in light of her father's example of a leadership lifestyle. The theme can be restated as the issue of leadership as a lifestyle encompassing instrumentation necessary to the way of interacting with others. As a transcendent theme, it does not move from the subconscious to be dealt with by the deliberate action of consciousness; rather, it arises as part of the practicality of assuming a career that is pervasive. Elizabeth's early family experience might have made it possible for her to more easily and quickly accommodate the necessity to work through the instrumentation issues arising from the leader role as pervading lifestyle. This way of being a leader was familiar; it was also implied in Anna's construction. Anna suggested this when she described the extent of her centeredness in the institutional domains. This is in further contrast to the leader role as compartmentalized and applying to the profession only.

Ellen

At the time Ellen came to the study, she had been president of her college for nearly three decades. The college was founded by the religious order she belonged to. As a young girl, Ellen had found the religious order compelling but decided to complete her college education before joining. Initially she had planned to return home and help with her younger siblings following undergraduate studies. Her goal was to "help with getting the younger children educated." She attributed the distress she felt at the idea of delaying entry into the convent to youthful exuberance or a need for immediacy. She joined the community at the age of 21 following her undergraduate work and prior to attending graduate school.

In 1952 she entered her order. Ellen was raised as a Catholic by her mother, who also grew up in that religion. Her father was Protestant but supported her mother's efforts to bring the Catholic religion and culture into their home. This upbringing was more than attending church on Sundays. It also meant observing holy days of obligation and other guiding tenets of that faith. The celebration of the faith took place both within and outside of her childhood home. Ellen attended Catholic schools as well. Her schoolday began with affirmation of her faith and individual classes also began with prayer.

The schools Ellen attended were places where she could excel in her academic work as well as gain mastery in organizing and leading in student government. She attended an all-girls' high school and continued her education in Catholic postsecondary schools. Ellen described herself as "always academically successful." Ellen admits to a general sense of ease in social contexts ranging from the home she shared with her parents and siblings to the schools she attended. The religious community she joined was seldom at odds with her sense of self. According to Ellen, "one of my greatest gifts in my life has been fitting in."

Ellen was the eldest of five children: four girls and one boy. She describes herself as someone with an affinity for the field of education. She found it to be exciting and energizing, a natural outlet for her desire to learn and to be a learned individual. She believed she would be a lifelong learner. Three of her siblings also entered education. Ellen's affinity for learning environments was encouraged by her parents, who were high school graduates and, as she described them, hard-working people. Her father worked as an electrician; her mother was a homemaker and active in local politics.

Ellen won a scholarship to attend college after graduating from high school in 1950. She became acquainted with the order she eventually joined during that time. She was taught Latin by the sisters. Ellen saw her order as the most significant factor in the development of her leader persona.

However, although her religious affiliation was central to her definition of self, the social contexts and historical moment were also important. Ellen grew up during a period that overlapped those providing contexts for Anna and Odette. The significant features were the gendered social roles and limited career opportunities for women. Teaching was available to women. At one time Ellen considered a career in nursing but settled on education instead.

Ellen was teaching at one of the order's schools when she was asked to pursue graduate studies. She described the experience:

> In the 1950s when I entered the [order], it was the responsibility of the people who are elected to be the governing group and they looked over those of us available for assignment. For example, we were told, "You teach in this school, you teach in that school, you nurse in that hospital." Our response was "thank you very much" and we went. That was part of vowing obedience. We accepted that. Nowdays it is different. Individuals have a lot of conversations and input into what they will do. Nobody ever said to me, "Would you like to study for a Ph.D. in English?"

Indeed, it seemed that religion was significant in Ellen's development as a leader. And it became so early in her life.

It is unusual to consider service and obedience as issues of transcendent themes related to instrumentation associated with the leadership role. Rather these are more likely to be viewed as practices growing out of the mission of sacred communities; for Ellen they were both.

Ellen was a child when the country entered World War II. Although the work force was comprised of more women than it was earlier in the century, she, like the other women of this study, was negotiating her way to adulthood in a larger social context. Ellen's immersion in religion distinguishes her developmental path. And it provided her with alternatives for the leader persona. She could draw upon women in the church who offered examples of leadership. Those women lead in tandem with priests in coexisting matriarchies and patriarchies. Each leads within domains circumscribed by the church and by their respective commitments to their religious communities.

When Ellen assumed leadership responsibilities as a young girl in primary and secondary school, she did not anticipate that she would one day lead an organization. Nor did she anticipate that she would be asked to head a medical facility sponsored by her community. When she entered her order, she was following a calling—a compulsion that drew her to her community and commitment. Overarching her developmental pathway was her desire to obey the dictates of a consciousness aligned with her faith. Faith became the foreground in the meaning she found in her life and what she hoped would be central to her contribution to people. Her motive for leading was submission to the life and responsibilities of her community. This differs from the women who took on leadership positions because they believed they brought particular abilities needed by their organizations.

Ellen did not report dramatic transforming experiences or events during the course of her early development. Nor did she seem to draw on models of men for constructions of leaders. Rather, the vows of her community became the principles governing her life. Moreover, Ellen's life as a religious provided her with models for leadership in her own and in other religious orders. To understand the nature of leadership and the construction of self as leader, Ellen could remain within the sectarian lifestyle she embraced.

Commitment to a religious life provided a lens through which Ellen's developmental pathway can be viewed. The transcendent theme Ellen occupied herself with at the time of the study was very much bound up in her religious life and instrumentation associated with the service and obedience. For her the issue was not whether to serve but how to ensure quality in her service as she carried out her responsibilities.

TRANSCENDENT THEMES AND INSTRUMENTATION IN THE PROCESS OF LEADING

This chapter was significant in that it suggests the importance of transcendent themes in the construction of the leader persona and in the way issues of instrumentation arise in the role and function of leadership. Transcendent themes may appear to be remote from identity development. Or, at best, they may appear to be indirectly related to other dynamics of identity formation, such as the organizing principle, early family cultural learning, and extrafamilial cultural learning and experiences. Nor do they emerge entirely independent of subconscious issues merging into consciousness. However, they are not longstanding subconscious ideations that have become insights; instead, they relate to instrumentation in the process of leading.

For example, Elizabeth grew up as an only child and as such enjoyed the kind of tutelage from her parents she might not have received had she grown up with siblings. She observed her father as leader in a variety of social contexts. Elizabeth's example of a transcendent theme is leadership as a lifestyle. She grew up observing her father as leader, and as such it was a pervasive role—a lifestyle. As a principal, his responsibilities extended beyond the school building into his community. Leadership as lifestyle could be a learned way of conceptualizing the role and all that it entails. To put it differently, it is conceivable to view it as such.

This learned conceptualization does not necessarily make it inevitable as an instrumentation issue. What is learned within family context can be mediated by exposure to extrafamiliar, divergent conceptualization. Prior learning makes leader-as-lifestyle, along with self-efficacy, a standard against which performance can be measured. This might also be considered in Ellen's case, where spiritual life and the responsibilities of secular leadership tasks have merged. Secular leadership tasks are distinguished here from spiritual leadership. Ellen's transcendent themes are service and obedience.

The transcendent themes of trust and advocacy are instrumentation issues with object relations defined within the leader role. These are significant for Isabella and Jessie as well. Standards for these relationships are set within both early family and extrafamilial contexts. As issues of instrumentation, the extrafamilial context becomes the focus. Transcendent themes seem to arise out of the consciousness, self-awareness. They facilitate the sense of efficacy and require a proactive response to address them in the ways that can be most productive.

5

The Esthetics of the Leader Persona and the Practice of Proaction and Self-Study

> "The social value of individuality is its uniqueness. Two people witnessing the same event fashion from their experiences building blocks that add to what are increasingly fundamental parts of who they are, further realization of their potential, and ultimately what they will become to others."

It is not surprising to find that our generalizations about people and statements of truths about the human condition do not hold up to tough scrutiny in most cases. As a result, generalizations must be qualified in some way, even when they are applied to a limited number of people. Individuals are intriguing in the way they challenge even our modest claims to understanding their being.

The next part of this discussion is more difficult and more risky than that offered earlier. It is my attempt to pull together the experiences of the women we have explored thus far and to offer a summary of the effect those experiences have had on their leader persona and to suggest ways of joining proaction with leadership theory and training. Although I took on this task at the outset, summarizing what I believe are the qualities that seem present in the way the women lead and relating those to the still emerging adult identity while not offering prescriptions remains a challenge.

As with the foregoing, this part of the discussion is conditioned on the premise that there is not an end point to identity formation. And although there are subtle and not-so-subtle influences that act on the subconscious mind to help shape their personas, individuals invent, construct, and co-construct features of their identity in deliberate, proactive ways.

This part of the discussion is risky because of the possibilities for individuals seeking alternative ways of approaching leadership to construe it as prescriptive as it describes the esthetics of the leader persona manifested in these women. My purpose would be defeated if the message becomes something that begins with "All good leaders . . . ," or "To be a good leader . . . ," or "Good leaders must . . ." I view this outcome as regressive. With the cautions noted, I will continue.

What I have described regarding the women in this discussion can be characterized as the esthetics of the leader persona, which seems to be products of the fusion of social contexts, phenomenological epistemological processes, and the translation of their products into behaviors. Those behaviors—that is, the practices referred to throughout this book as instrumentation—are brought to bear on transactions, the moment-to-moment, day-to-day encounters between individuals with formal assignments to the leader roles and individuals serving as leaders through the leadership function.

THE ESTHETICS OF THE LEADER PERSONA DEFINED

Esthetics here refers to the impressions associated with the leader's way of being. It is in part perception as well. Therefore, in total, esthetics is the overall quality of the leader persona perceived by others. Esthetics as a product of influences within psychosocial development is particularly visible in the instrumentation of leadership. However, without relying solely on instrumentation for evidence, it is also possible to find it in the vivid examples offered by the women. Those examples will be considered in global terms and again later more specifically.

Social context has been significant in this consideration of identity formation and the leader persona. Context refers to the circumstances that act upon identity. It teaches rules composed through social interaction and normed against a myriad of conditions. Gendered roles defining masculinity and femininity are among those norms. Within those constructions, the parameters applied to those roles dictate personal and professional lifestyle as well as interpersonal and institutional arrangements.

Although self-study is a characteristic of identity achievement, the willingness of the women to be engaged in protracted discussion of their ascendency to leader positions was helpful. Their ability to juxtapose themselves in relationship to the tasks at hand and to individuals involved in or associated with their organizations lends a significant quality to their way of being a leader. That positioning circumscribes identities and treatments of others in the organization. It builds a rationale for object relations and serves as one of the bases for resolving issues of effective instrumentation. That the counsel to "know thyself" makes the design of productive and mutually satisfying relationships eminently more attainable is not a startling revelation. This self-knowledge is widely accepted as a positive feature and outcome of the maturation process. As an ideal, it ranks high among the standards that drive searches for a mature individual to lead. This is in contrast to an individual who is developing as a leader—this might be stated in terms of future potential.

Identity development and self-study are continuous processes. The emphasis is on the continuation of growth. The esthetics is associated with the progressive development of these women and accommodated their ascendency to leader roles. Although their identity work was highly visible, their credibility was not undermined. The women seemed to be confident in their roles. Social rules governing the lives of women permitted the appearance of active engagement in the kind of self-study that could have been construed as exhibitions of inadequacy or a stereotypical "soft" side to the leader persona. There was evidence of an effect on reconciliation of prescribed ways of being, on idealized functioning, on the phenomenological epistemological process, and on the translation of their products to instrumentation.

Instrumentation issues can be, and are often, resolved through subscription to prescribed approaches to carrying out the responsibilities of the leadership role. Those approaches are behavior-based and attempt to illicit a reciprocal response from individuals in the organizational community. Examples of this might be the use of sanctions to ensure compliance with production standards. In service organizations, they could be protocols for intake of clients. In education, they might dictate student and teacher or parent and teacher interactions. This applies in adult and postsecondary school communities as well.

Behavior approaches are distinguishable from the combination of transactional, cognitive, and analytical exchanges ventured into without trepidation or with some concern but nonetheless in pursuit of the dialectical encounter.

THE CONVERGENCE OF CONFERRED IDENTITY AND PROFESSIONAL CONSTRUCTIONS

Along the developmental pathway, the individual encounters ways of being: cultural traditions, values, ideations, and transactional rules, parts of which become distilled to their essence. Those essential qualities are relative to individuals' perceiving and then constructing meaning. Getting to their essence and making sense of what has been captured takes shape as tests and comparisons with the interpretation of both internal and external worlds conferred on individuals by their families. The major ingredient of change during the development of the individual is the efflorescence of dissonance upon encounters with new contexts. The learning continues and, in the case of the women described here, there arises the need for a professional persona, an aspect of identity designed to function within individually set parameters.

As suggested earlier, the esthetics of the leader persona seems to be a product of the struggle to become—whether subtle, as in the case of Anna and Elizabeth, or more dramatic, as in the case of Samillia and Odette. Constructions of professional identity are less ways of being to aspire to than they are qualitative aspects of individuals' identities that ultimately influence the ways in which leader roles are managed. Consequently, they influence the domain of experiences that are dependent on or subject to those roles. Thus the esthetics associated with the women were as individual as their leader personas.

The social value of individuality is its uniqueness. Two people witnessing the same event fashion from their experiences building blocks that add to what are increasingly fundamental parts of who they are, further realization of their potential, and ultimately what they will become to others. The influence of an event on the lives of those who experience it is exponential in its contribution to the development of ways of being. There are throughout lifetimes many contributions and inputs that constitute identities. Thus it may be said that those variations are historically derived.

PHENOMENOLOGICAL EPISTEMOLOGICAL PROCESSES

Self-study suggests a proactive course under circumstances made fertile by insights. Contemporary, conventional wisdom regarding leadership and instrumentation issues argues "Leader, know thyself." To know oneself involves refocusing of the inquiry into the relationship between leadership and the organization. Recent discussions, this one included, support a match between organizations and individuals. An earlier wisdom advised, "Leader know thy organization." This focus was on the organization as a functional structure according to its expressed purpose. It might be added that this particular way of positioning the aspiring leader within the organization was instrumentation and largely concerned with production. Production as the center of life in the organization was implicit in this way of being. Interaction among members of the community as a source of self-efficacy and affirmation was not of concern for the leader under this circumscribed conceptualization of the leader persona.

To know oneself is more than an understanding in the moment requiring a particular instrumentation. It is to know how the "I" was conceived and ultimately constructed, to anticipate the juxtaposition of "I" in light of that construction, and to reshape a way of being. The individual in the moment resets parameters of her identity. She moves from beginning insights to what might seem to be limits of who she is and considers possibilities. Throughout this immersion, as it was referred to earlier, there are both acquisitive and dispossessive dynamics of the psychology of the leader persona in operation.

Samillia, Odette, and Ellen are striking examples of this. Samillia's rejection of traditions governing the lives of women in her cultures (her family and a broader ethnic culture) was provocative for the people of those cultures. She anticipated it would be, as she pushed past constraints on her identity. The process was given volition in the questions preceding it: What else can I be? What else do I want to be? What am I willing to dispossess to acquire a different way of being? Dispossession here refers to modification as well as rejection of cultural prescriptions. There were requirements for fulfillment within cultural norms. Samillia's baseline for actively constructing her leader persona was contained within those norms.

The points of contrast she experienced outside of her family were references for being different. Within those contrasts, she could begin to answer the questions posed. As suggested earlier, each answer tested for its ability to ground and provide a sense of self-efficacy. Self-efficacy as a factor influencing the esthetics of the leader persona can be viewed as trust and confidence in one's ability to pose and then answer questions of identity. This is confidence in one's ability to find the process of development meaningful. This dialectical process is necessarily subjective. Consequently, individual proaction is subjective. The phenomenological epistemological processes—self-study as an influence on the esthetics—is the experience of the observer rather than that of the individuals observed.

Samillia's self-study was motivated by the contrast she experienced in what seemed to her at times divergent cultures and her sense of the inequities between the roles of men and those of women. These became the issues that helped to shape the questions she posed regarding her identity. The upper limits of her achievement, according to her family culture, was set as wife and mother within a lifestyle grounded in her ethnicity and gendered within that larger set of values and norms. Samillia's exploration of other possibilities changed boundaries set earlier in her life. She chose to extricate herself from the roles acceptable for women.

Samillia's proactive identity formation was oppositional to the interfamilial design, which changed from girl-mother to woman-student, nongendered friend, colleague, and leader—to name a few of the possibilities that became available to her. She was not constrained by these. For her, they were not incompatibly discrete states; rather, she could experience them simultaneously. These aspects of identity are accessible in contexts that were not generative of them. In this way her leader persona was not a character put on to meet the needs of the moment.

Phenomenological epistemological processes, also dialectical in nature, raise consciousness in ways that might be likened to the interactive thera- peutic group process. Individuals within the organization can be and often are part of the experience of self-exploration. Both Elizabeth and Jessie suggested this in their description of issues they faced regarding confidants and trust. The benefits of those kinds of relationships included feedback on object relations within the context of leading and leader influence on institutional culture and protocols.

Ellen brings another dimension to the exploration of self, conscious- ness-raising, and development of the leader persona. Defining boundaries included her commitment to her parents and to religious practices that governed her life globally. As a result of her affiliation with members of her order, she took on her religious grounding as a lifestyle. What she was and wanted to be were in part prescribed and understood by her as per- sonal and spiritual growth as a member of that community.

Ellen's explorations of identity possibilities were bound to her vows and the extent to which she could attain the ideal spiritual state. That state included some of the following ways of being: to show compassion, to see all life as worthy of God's love, to continuously seek understanding, to look forward to complete being in the spiritual presence of God. These aspira- tions coupled with the press of the material world focused her study of self. Ellen's consciousness-raising was deliberately spiritual. The artifacts of the growth were the roles she took on in service to life and thus to God. Her development as a leader was the corollary of devotion to her commu- nity and what it represented. Secular challenges were opportunities for spiritual maturation. This was an awareness Ellen embraced.

The esthetics of the leader persona is also embodied in the accessibility of developmental experiences, the accommodation of self-exploration, and the disclosure and ease represented in the confidence and poise these indi- viduals expressed. There is more to the total impression of these women, which can best be described here as a further influence of leader esthetics.

THE INFLUENCE OF SOCIAL CONTEXTS ON THE EMERGENCE OF THE LEADER ESTHETICS

Another influence on the emergence of the leader esthetics seems to be social contexts. All of the women provided vivid descriptions of the way their environments at various periods of their lives influenced their devel- opment. They were able to perceive themselves as capable of leading. They assumed positions that provided opportunities to test their self-perceptions and their skills. Those experiences facilitated application of their organizing principles. For example, Anna's beliefs about social inequities and justice were put to the test when she organized and led groups to disobey segregation laws by participating in the civil rights movement.

Samillia tested her beliefs on similar issues when she took assignments that required her to organize members of African-American and Hispanic communities to act in their interests for schooling for themselves and their children. In both of these examples, there seemed to be paths for emergence of the advocacy feature of their leader persona. They served as advocates on behalf of people rather than in the more traditional role of paladin for the production function exemplars of leadership.

In another example, Jessie abandoned her family's expectation that she would construct a lifestyle for herself within its acceptable gendered traditions of being a wife and mother and pursuing employment suitable for women. Like Samillia, Jessie contrasted familial context with the kinds of experiences she had during her schooling and employment. Because of the gendered prescriptions for women's lives during their early developmental periods, it is not surprising that these women had to surmount both private and public expectations of them. To do so, it was necessary for them to seek novel experiences and responsibilities that were considered risky for women. They had stepped outside of the lives framed for them.

Through the experiences they sought out, the women were able to explore the use of power. As part of the leader esthetics, they tended to approach the use of power in unconventional ways. As a convention, power differentials were used in favor of higher-level positions. However, the women engaged in synergistic uses of power.

This use included sharing leadership functions. Recall that the distinction is between the role and the function: The leader role is a formal designation and the function is an assignment of responsibilities that might traditionally be associated with that role. For example, college presidents are their institutions' fund-raisers. However, representatives may be sent to events instead. In that capacity, the function of the leader is shared. In another instance, an individual might act on behalf of the chief executive at administrative meetings. The synergy in these assignments is realized in the gain in individual competency, self-efficacy, and self-determinism in career path. This influence on the esthetics is tempering. There is a mindfulness in the individual that is experienced as intangible but presents qualities during encounters with the women. The synergy, the return and increase in power seemed to be in the form of personal and professional freedom. The women relinquished control to gain a courageous spirit. They were mindful of their leadership. To be mindful then is to "be" in the circumstance and state of one's organizational community: to live it in connected ways.

The apparent ease with which this seemed to eventually happen for these women emerges from the resolutions of issues arising in the self-defining process. In some instances, these included the dilemmas of masculine and feminine dichotomies encountered in both familial and social contexts. Samillia's pattern was adherence, rejection, partial syntheses, and some compromise that included possibilities not available to women according to her orienting culture. The synthesis in regard to her leader persona was a combination of what were for her functional and philosophical approaches to working with people. The dominant feature of the syntheses was women's ways of nurturing. The origins of that feature were her experiences as a caregiver.

Ellen provides a uniquely different example. Her developmental goals were at once her own and those of the religious community to which she belonged. They were aspirations that moved into her consciousness early in her life and that were grounded in her relationships with her parents and siblings. She was dedicated to her parents and positioned herself to support them by caring for her younger siblings. In another individual, this might have been perceived as the course of a shy, retiring young woman secluding herself from extrafamilial experiences. Ellen's choices were not those of an individual lacking a sense of connectedness to her peers. She was popular as a young girl, she was socially responsive, and she obligated herself to assume leader responsibilities. Those responsibilities began early in her life and continued as part of her calling in her religious life.

For Ellen, there was a merger of her life with her family and within her order. She grew up in the church and committed herself to service (raising her siblings with her parents). Through her calling she merged service, belonging to community, and vocation. In a very real sense, leading was part of Ellen's calling. As a result, providing a more complete view of her context requires going beyond the definitions provided by popular culture—as represented in scripts, text, or subtext—and championed by groups or individuals with whom she might identify. Although influenced by those, she became aware of one transcendental lifestyle, which she embraced as a religious.

As a religious, Ellen's use of power differentials is governed by her vows. Consequently, her esthetics necessarily resolves the dichotomy between power over and empowerment. While she acknowledges her leader task, she works in collaboration with the other members of her community as well as with those she serves. Ellen's vows and the mission of her order moderate her use of power. Regarding power, the founder of her order set the example of lifestyle and organizing principles as a religious.

Power was used to enable mapping of individual and community goals. Ellen's commitment positioned her to serve. Her assumption of leader positions was unprivileged, clothed in humility, and a feature of unparalleled tenderness unrelated to condescension. Because of this there seemed to be an early reconciliation of issues that might create tensions and ultimately the kind of dissonance that could shake the foundations of individual identity.

With the compatibility of purpose, career, lifestyle, and ideology, for Ellen the tensions experienced were largely related to degree of accomplishment in service. The tension she experienced seemed to be creative rather than frenetic. For an example of this, she referred to the occasion when she was asked to assume different responsibilities. Her concerns were related to optimizing her ability to minister to the needs of her community.

THE FUSION OF SOCIAL CONTEXTS

As an influence on the leader esthetics, the fusion of social contexts may be more accurately presented in the examples as coalescence of intrapsychic process influencing a way of being. This is essentially meaning-making with associated tasks brought to bear on individual position. It is, as argued earlier, a juxtapositioning of events, personal history, and organizational or community cultures. The individual encounters are with the organizational consciousness. The process governing that encounter is transactional. Recall the discussion of the leader's treatment of the other. Transaction was defined as including mutuality of purposes and expectations within assignment of formal and informal roles. The use of power differentials is also transactional in nature. The leader esthetics mediates the transaction as well.

Phenomenological epistemological processes, intrapsychic effects, and the ways of experiencing and adapting to social context are only a few of the influences on the leader esthetics. Another influence is the translation of self-study and understanding or meaning-making to behaviors and ways of leading.

The description of the influences on the esthetics are familiar, since they are the results of maturation in identity development. They can be placed within the exploration and emergent dynamics, insights and coming to consciousness. One can see the influence of the organizing principles in particular in the construction of the leader persona and consequently on the esthetics. The leader persona acts on social institutions, making significant contributions to the way they function, what people of those institutions value, and what they define as their mission and purpose.

Moreover, the character of leadership guides institutional practice. The translations of those products into behaviors were first presented here as transcendent themes. Tensions exist in those themes; primary among them, for example, was the issue of being "separate from" or "part of" in relating to others as members of organizational communities. This was expressed as the relationship of "I" to the "other," redefinition of social context, and reconciliation of dissonance. There are others that were presented earlier.

The constellation of these influences supports the impression of these women as competent and highly adaptive. This impression is significant because of the proposition that leadership is largely transactional. The modification to that proposition is that the adaptive leader may be better able to engage in those transactions in ways that are mutually beneficial. The leader benefits, as do the members of the organizational community, as well as the organizational structure. The leader and others are engaged in orienting communication from exchange to exchange. As a result, viewpoints are modified, facilitating the changes and shifts in organizational purpose. The relationship between the leader persona and institution is dynamic in its nature. The events surrounding communication and ways of being come together to influence not only organizational context, but those beyond the immediate sphere of influence.

In one instance, it is possible that caregiving falls within the domain of reasonable and acceptable responses for leaders. Arguably this emerges from the gendered socialization of women who become leaders. Consequently, caring or caregiving in the institutional context takes the form of concern for career development, career pathways, focus on the use of power differentials, assignment of leader responsibilities, and consultative decision making. The goal shifts between object relations as the primary task and competency and personal development secondarily. Trust also presents as a theme requiring expression in instrumentation. The behavioral expressions of the leader persona become incorporated as acceptable ways of interacting.

There is a synchronicity of attitudes among the individuals in the organization and those of the leader persona. This is an alignment of ways of being within a community. Along with acceptance of transactional idiosyncrasy, the behavioral expression normed by leadership are assimilated by others. For example, caring is expressed in consonant behaviors. Statements of caring with unnormed behaviors are likely to be viewed as aberrant and cause tension-creating dissonance.

Other examples include hiring practices and project development. Both are, of course, instrumentation areas. Beginning with hiring practices, review, and contract renewal, an institution can ensure at the very minimum compatibility of values with regard to its identity and its goals, although agreement can also result from the psychology of cognitive dissonance. If agreement results from the dialectic of exploration, the organization's values and reconciliation as described in identity development with non-significant variation in compatibility can be sustained.

If agreement results from sublimation or repression, it is likely that differences believed to be irreconcilable will surface. In this case disengagement must be addressed—if not by the individual, then by the institution. This is not the stuff of "attitude adjustment"; one can overlook significant differences in what the leader values and what the organization values. Psychological defenses emerge to extricate or rescue the individual. This is the decision to move on.

Organizations rely on procedures to press their issues. In business organizations, a contract may not be renewed. In educational organizations, junior faculty may not receive tenure. For most people, it is probably difficult to sustain the appearance of compatibility. To put it cynically, it is not always possible to sustain a pretense indefinitely. There is also the case of separation, when the individual discovers later in her development that she has grown apart from the organization.

To accomplish the work of the organization, to meet its goals, personnel must understand and support them through project development. The support must be mutual among members of the community vital to the project's implementation. Leadership sets the tone in order for support to coalesce. Expressions without consistent behavior could also be experienced as insincere or manipulative or at best symbolic, particularly in the absence of synchronicity of the leader persona with the organizational community.

Another way of considering this dynamic is to frame it as issues of congruence among individuals. From this perspective, the institution's leadership maintains its influence in shaping goals, norms, and purpose. Individuals seeking entry and standing to participate in the life of that community must find its work and direction acceptable. Acceptability is defined here as not being in complete opposition ideologically and functionally. This definition does not require total agreement or commitment. Rather, dissonance remains a significant factor in the ability of individuals to adapt to the institutional culture. The use of congruence instead of synchronicity acknowledges divergent meaning systems that accommodate each other.

Areas of divergence are not fatal for the relationship. The question might be posed: If the relationship is synchronic, is it also congruent? One response seems to be that this is a way of reconciling the two states if they are more similar than dissimilar. However, where there are ideological and functional differences that are fatal, it follows that the relationship is incompatible.

The term *identity congruence* offers a more vivid explanation of the nonfatal divergence of meaning systems. For example, Odette was able to compartmentalize her leader persona by applying definitions of *masculine* and *feminine* taken from popular culture. She was able to adapt and saw herself as not being compromised. The distinctions she perceived in her career persona and private life persona were not fatal to her institutional relationships. Later, this adaptation became less tenable.

In another example, Ellen's life as a religious was synchronous with the way she perceived herself prior to entering her order. The choice for her was to serve as a religious rather than as a layperson. As with the entire cycle of adult identity development, adaptation of the aspects of these perspectives influenced instrumentation and the translation of the earlier process into behaviors.

The instrumentation influences on the esthetics of the leader persona can be contrasted in the following:

- Synergistic use of power versus posturing
- Community focus versus "I" or individual focus
- Consultative decision making versus unilateral, authoritarian, and dictatorial approaches
- Transactions defined as reconciliation of meaning; systems versus adversarial positioning

Additional influences on the esthetics include: Encouragement of organizational culture, which encourages congruence and synchronicity, caring and caregiving in the institutional context as an organizational norm, focus on ethical use of power differentials, sharing leader responsibilities, shifts between object relations as the primary task and competency and personal development secondarily, and trust as a theme in instrumentation. These are listed to provide contrast rather than arguing a comparison of functional and dysfunctional styles in leadership.

Leadership is central to organizational functioning, including perseverance in its purpose and in realization of its goals. The training of new leaders focuses on more experienced individuals for their wisdom and what are most likely to be prescriptive ways of leading. To that end, this discussion has attempted to bring into the foreground the role of identity development aspects of individuals which emerge in the role as the leader persona.

Proaction in the design of the leader persona offers possibilities for an adaptive and ultimately interpersonally resourceful individual to assume leadership. However, with proaction as a central issue to the developmental status emergence, there also comes to the forefront the issue of authenticity of character. In this instance, character refers to the carriage of the leader persona. Although it has been addressed here extensively, the possibility of feeling fraudulent in the persona of the leader arises as the need to be genuine in her approach to members of the organizational community.

This may be part of the orienting experience of individuals coming to new organizations and new careers. Such transitions may be mildly traumatic, precipitating immersion, self-exploration, and the testing of organizing principles. The sense of being inauthentic may be indicative of the transitional phase (a return to moratorium) and serve as a catalyst for addressing unresolved identity issues.

PROACTION IN THE DESIGN OF THE LEADER PERSONA

The influences on the esthetics of the leader persona come together as an overall impression of the individual. The leader identity can be an area of intervention. Consequently, these influences can be cultivated during the process of intervention.

The persona as a constructed feature of identity takes into consideration self-determination; the influence of organizing principles and values on instrumentation; and developmental pathways, which include interfamilial and extrafamilial experiences. As the individual is expressive of the related interpsychic states, her way of being necessarily reflects balances in emergent stages of object relations.

The leader persona as an aspect of the individual psyche is unique. It is bound up in an individual's process of becoming. The benefit of focusing on proaction in the design of the leader persona is the possibility of refining relevant meaning-making, making sense of continually changing circumstances, and acquiring appropriate behavioral responses. This makes following rules for getting people to work toward the function of the organizational community simplistic. Recall that the premise of proaction includes leadership as part of psychosocial development and assumes the changeability of individuals in response to social contexts. Individuals' past, present, and future act upon life in organizations. Accordingly, leadership training shifts to the individual and guided or facilitated by self-study.

The implications for leadership training on curricula in light of the foregoing discussion are not extremely dramatic. However, they do involve an emphasis on individual psychology. This is self-study of the points of intersection for the individual and the organization. It also includes development of the ability to be mindful.

In discussions of leadership, descriptions of instrumentation dominate. The process of engagement provides a compelling topic or focus for training. The framing sessions typically include exposure of personality traits and behavioral practice for the purpose of acquisition; the presentation in total assumes that the individual who is capable of leading should be given a store of resources. A particular personality trait becomes a single aspiration, unintegrated into the total leader persona apart form the circumstances deeming it an appropriate tool. For example, if it is the rule that a particular context is amenable to a charismatic trait, then one would practice until one, at the very least, is able to gain a close approximation of that trait. What comes naturally to some individuals is a comfortable, context-dependent garment for others. This is familiar in the developmental history of some of the women presented here. If circumstances require an emotionally distant response, then the character is played as the stoic, emphasizing the intellectual approach that better serves the context.

There is flexibility in these characterizations. However, the change-ability of character-as-leadership practice requires the skill of actors. And, unfortunately, there may very well be a belief that thespians are better leaders. Consequently, the shift to adult identity development is a dramatic change in the culture of leadership training.

Still, there are those who might argue in favor of the short-term effect produced by team-building experiences. Participants in those courses report epiphanies—moments of enlightenment in which they see themselves more clearly, as well as the consequences of their actions and the possibility of creating ideal working relationships. One must ask how practical is a trek to the local obstacle course for the requisite experience leading to individuals' bonding around a particular job in order to become productive.

It is difficult to predict which experience will bring on the transformation. Free-falling blindfolded from a 6-foot platform might serve as a catalyst for some individuals. Propelling off the top of a 14-foot pole may do it for others. Mountain climbing, spelunking, surfing, and perhaps even bungee-jumping may provide a sufficient surge of psychic energy to kick in a moment of enlightenment.

Although it would be perhaps unfair to totally discount such experiences as catalysts for self-study, they pay only passing attention to the phenomenon of adult identity development or identity development over one's lifetime, despite the premise that epiphany equates with coming to consciousness and insights. In addition, these are not gender-neutral experiences; rather, they are bound to the socially constructed dichotomies of masculine and feminine. These are activities appropriated as part of masculine experiences and ways of building character. They are not necessarily designed to develop insights into the need to cultivate emotional intelligence, for example. Rather, the epiphany is grand, stirring the spirit and bringing out the mythical warrior.

Along with prescriptive leadership, one might consider ways in which leadership boot camp could benefit from the shift to the phenomenological approach without feminizing it and giving rise to another co-opted, hackneyed phrase similar to "politically correct leader training." Yet another issue arises regarding the shift—the possibility of combining the adrenaline rush that has been popular for at least a decade with the approaches to proaction in identity development. There are three distinct components to this issue: (1) the addition of proaction; (2) the perspective of proaction as facilitative of identity development without an end point; (3) the philosophical shift in emphasis as to what constitutes leadership and the leader persona.

For a look at proaction from the perspective of the individual and the other as facilitator, the influences on the leader esthetics are useful. They serve as points of reference or beginning points. As such, they are phenomenological epistemological processes—accessibility of developmental experiences, the fusion of social contexts, and the translation of self-study and understanding to behaviors.

Treating proaction as facilitative of identity development without an end point presses the individual to view herself as not inclined to reach a point of stasis. Rather, each encounter, from moment to moment, day to day, provides focal points for the dialectic involved in the process of becoming.

From this understanding of self, the individual is able to more securely turn her focus outward in the encounter with others. Those encounters are benign with regard to the challenges to her ego. Instead of defensive posturing during engagement with the other and what is essentially unknown, there can be a mutually beneficial encounter. This is part of the "mindful" state of being in leadership. It is not, however, hypervigilance, a state that anticipates catastrophe and thus problematizes present and future encounters.

The third issue is the most significant. It is part of the other two. It is also an issue that has been of concern since someone pointed out that the individual directing their hunting-and-gathering lifestyle was also their leader. This is not intended to be disparaging, nor is it intended to be the definitive statement on all that is known of the history of sentience. What constitutes leadership is seldom answered with regard to the persona of the individual leading. It is addressed primarily through instrumentation.

Not only are the skills expected of the individual subsumed under this category; so, too, is the individual herself. As a result, *leader, leading,* and *instrumentation* are synonymous. It may be possible to achieve a philosophical shift in definition by distinguishing each of these. To a large extent, that has been the task at hand. The shift would create the possibility for change ranging from minimally emphasizing the influence each has on a discrete process to extensive study of each as integral to the enterprise of leadership.

Exploration of leadership would, therefore, cover what one brings to the task in terms of one's psychology, identity development, cultivation of sensitivity and ability for self-study and monitoring, store of useful approaches to instrumentation, and the organization as a community.

Even with this, there remains the question of what constitutes leadership. There are several reasons for this. One that seems to beg the question is nonetheless offered here. The question is rhetorical and, therefore, the attempt to answer it is a heuristic. A response like the leader persona is influenced by social context, the needs of the organizational community giving rise to the need for a leader, and what the individual who would lead, along with those who would be led, bring to the encounter in which all stand poised for engagement.

In many respects this discussion might be read as calling for those who would aspire to be leaders as well as those who are leading to be overly self-conscious and self-involved. Clearly there is always the risk that what starts out as a possibility for change instead becomes an extreme and counterproductive response.

TOWARD DEVELOPING A PRACTICE OF PROACTION AND SELF-STUDY

Individuals are remarkable in the amount of energy they often put into development of their cognitive skills. The change from prescriptive leadership to a focus on continuous development and an adaptive leader persona is no less a challenge and also requires expenditures of large amounts of psychological energy. According to the suggestions here, the way one knows oneself in relation to others and the way one encounters meaning systems—whether they are acquired through family orienting experiences (untested) or constructed through dialectics (tested)—involves a mindfulness that may generally not be part of one's psychological repertoire.

Even when individuals encounter obviously new and different social experiences, they may take for granted that they encounter features of realities similar to their own and act accordingly. As a result, there is a sense of knowing that, notwithstanding differences, accommodation and a meaningful exchange can take place. Although this may be so at some level, it risks imposing a dominant interpretation on the communication unfolding. This is especially so where one comes to the interaction as leader. It assumes an adjustment of subordinate to dominant. The energy expended is unbalanced, with the subordinate struggling to accommodate. Reciprocity may be intended, but it is not facilitated by imposition of a dominant interpretation.

A behavior example will help to demonstrate this point. When individuals are first learning a set of behaviors intended to produce a specific outcome, they are meticulous about performing each step toward their goal. Eventually, as they become more familiar with the steps they must take toward their goal, the inclination to conserve energy imposes limits on their activity. Those individuals begin to anticipate each next step and each outcome. From this point on, they also make decisions about the value of each step in the series they must take to reach their goal. Some steps become tertiary and eventually superfluous. They are discontinued. As this conservation begins to take place, the quality of the outcome changes. Conservation of energy intended to boost outcome becomes nonproductive.

During the experience of changing one's thinking, the tendency may be to conserve psychological energy, to assume understanding of one's own as well as others' motives, to assume that one fully comprehends the other. Rather than being vulnerable and actively seeking to gain insights, one opts for conservation, allowing counterproductive defense mechanisms to dominate interaction. Such conservation makes it difficult to be a student and thus cultivate intelligences—such as emotional and social perceptiveness, and perhaps dharma and spirituality, for example. It allows counterproductive defense mechanisms to dominate interaction.

The altered state that comes with being a learner can be blunted through the act of compensation, an example of a defense mechanism. Women who put on a masculine way of being in order to make up for their gendered socialization stand to lose the possibility of shifting from hierarchical leadership practice to a partnership of organization members.

References

Astin, H. S., & Leland, C. (1991). *Women of influence, women of vision: A cross-generational study of leaders and social change.* San Francisco: Jossey-Bass.

Belenky, M. F., Clinchy, B. M., Goldberger, N. R., & Tarule, J. M. (1986). *Women's ways of knowing: The development of self, voice, and mind.* New York: Basic Books.

Bennis, W. (1989). *On becoming a leader.* New York: Addison-Wesley.

Bennis, W. (1991). *Why leaders can't lead: The unconscious conspiracy continues.* San Francisco: Jossey-Bass.

Birnbaum, R. (1992). *How academic leadership works: Understanding success and failure in the college presidency.* San Francisco: Jossey-Bass.

Blase, J., & Anderson, G. L. (1995). *The micropolitics of educational leadership: From control to empowerment.* New York: Teachers College Press.

Chodorow, N. J. (1989). *Feminism and psychoanalytic theory.* New Haven, CT: Yale University Press.

Chodorow, N. J. (1994). *Femininities, masculinities, sexualities: Freud and beyond.* Lexington: University Press of Kentucky.

Collins, P. H. (1990). *Black feminist thought: Knowledge, consciousness, and the politics of empowerment.* New York: Routledge.

DuBrin, A. J. (1995). *Leadership: Research findings, practice, and skills.* Boston: Houghton Mifflin.

Ferguson, K. E. (1984). *The feminist case against bureaucracy.* Philadelphia: Temple University Press.

Gardner, J. W. (1990). *On leadership.* New York: Free Press.

Gilligan, C. (1982). *In a different voice: Psychological theory and women's development.* Cambridge, MA: Harvard University Press.

Greene, M. (1978). *Landscapes of learning.* New York: Teachers College Press.

Greene, M. (1988). *The dialectic of freedom.* New York: Teachers College Press.

Harding, S. (1991). *Whose science? Whose knowledge?: Thinking from women's lives.* Ithaca, NY: Cornell University Press.

Helgesen, S. (1990). *The female advantage: Women's ways of leadership.* New York: Doubleday Currency.

Hunt, J. (1984). Organizational leadership: The contingency paradigm and its challenges. In B. Kellerman (Ed.), *Leadership: Multidisciplinary perspectives* (pp. 113–138). Englewood Cliffs, NJ: Prentice-Hall.

Irigaray, L. (1985). *This sex which is not one.* Ithaca, NY: Cornell University Press.

Jacobson, S., & Conway, J. (1990). *Educational leadership in an age of reform*. New York: Longman.

Jaggar, A., & Rothenberg, P. (1993). *Feminist frameworks: Alternative theoretical accounts of the relations between women and men* (3rd ed.). New York: McGraw-Hill.

Janeway, E. (1990). Women and the uses of power. In H. Eisenstein & A. Jardine (Eds.), *The future of difference* (pp. 327–344). New Brunswick, NJ: Rutgers University Press.

Josselson, R. (1990). *Finding herself: Pathways to identity development in women*. San Francisco: Jossey-Bass.

Josselson, R. (1992). *The space between us: Exploring the dimensions of human relationships*. San Francisco: Jossey-Bass.

Kegan, R. (1982). *The evolving self: Problem and process in human development*. Cambridge, MA: Harvard University Press.

Kegan, R. (1994). *In over our heads*. Cambridge, MA: Harvard University Press.

Kotter, J. P. (1988). *The leadership factor*. New York: Free Press.

Kouzes, J., & Posner, B. (1996). *The leadership challenge: How to get extraordinary things done in organizations*. New York: Jossey-Bass.

Laidlaw, T. A., & Malmo, C. (1990). *Healing voices: Feminist approaches to therapy with women*. San Francisco: Jossey-Bass.

Marcia, J. E. (1993). The ego identity status approach to ego identity. In J. E. Marcia, A. S. Waterman, D. R. Matteson, S. L. Archer, & J. L. Orlofsky (Eds.), *Ego identity: A handbook for psychosocial research* (pp. 22–41). New York: Springer-Verlag.

Marcia, J. E., Waterman, A. S., Matteson, D. R., Archer, S. L., & Orlofsky, J. L. (1993). *Ego identity: A handbook for psychosocial research*. New York: Springer-Verlag.

Maxcy, S. (1991). *Educational leadership: A critical pragmatic perspective*. New York: Bergin & Garvey.

Messinger, R. (1990). Women in power and politics. In H. Eisenstein & A. Jardine (Eds.), *The future of difference* (pp. 318–326). New Brunswick, NJ: Rutgers University Press.

Mills, C. W. (1993). The structure of power in American society. In M. Olsen & M. Marger (Eds.), *Power in modern societies* (pp. 161–169). San Francisco: Westview.

Morrison, A. M. (1992). *The new leaders: Guidelines on leadership diversity in America*. San Francisco: Jossey-Bass.

Odden, A. R. (1995). *Educational leadership for America's schools*. New York: McGraw-Hill.

Rosaldo, R. (1993). *Culture and truth: The remaking of social analysis*. Boston: Beacon.

Vroom, V. H., & Jago, A. G. (1988). *The new leadership: Managing participation in organizations*. Englewood Cliffs, NJ: Prentice-Hall.

Waterman, A. S. (1993). Developmental perspectives on identity formation: From adolescence to adulthood. In J. E. Marcia, A. S. Waterman, D. R. Matteson, S. L. Archer, & J. L. Orlofsky (Eds.), *Ego identity: A handbook for psychosocial research* (pp. 42–68). New York: Springer-Verlag.

Watkins, G. (1989). *Talking back: Thinking feminist, thinking back, bell hooks.* Boston: South End Press.

Weedon, C. (1987). *Feminist practice and poststructuralist theory.* Oxford, UK: Basil Blackwell.

Weisstein, N. (1994). Kinder, Kuche, Kirche as scientific law: Psychology constructs the female. In M. Schneir (Ed.), *Feminism in our time: The essential writings, World War II to the present* (pp. 213–228). New York: Vintage.

Yekovich, F. (1993). A theoretical view of the development of expertise in credit administration. In P. Hallinger, K. Leithwood, & J. Murphy (Eds.), *Cognitive perspectives on educational leadership* (pp. 146–166). New York: Teachers College Press.

Yukl, G. A. (1989). *Leadership in organizations.* Englewood Cliffs, NJ: Prentice-Hall.

Index

Adaptive leaders, 95
Anderson, G. L., 19
Anna, 33–36, 43, 56
　career history, 33–34, 54
　education history, 33, 54, 61
　family history, 34–36, 41, 48–50, 53–54, 55, 59, 61, 62
　leader persona, 48–50, 53–55, 59, 60, 65, 92
Archer, S. L., 22
Astin, H. S., 13, 16
Attribute theories of leadership, 12–13

Belenky, Mary F., x, 24
Bennis, W., 10
Birnbaum, R., 8
Blase, J., 19

Chodorow, N. J., 16
Clinchy, B. M., 24
Collins, P. H., 15
Constructivist leadership
　Anna, 33–36, 41, 43, 48–50, 53–55, 56, 59–62, 65, 92
　and construction of self as leader, x
　context in, 59–63
　Elizabeth, 77–81, 84–85
　Ellen, 82–84, 85, 91, 93–94
　emergence of concept, 16–19
　identity development and, x, 17–19, 27–28
　Isabella, 73–77, 85
　Jessie, 69–73, 85, 91, 92
　leader persona and. See Leader persona

methodology of study, 29–30
Odette, 36–40, 41–42, 55–61, 62, 64
reciprocity in, ix–x
Samillia, 30–33, 40–41, 50–53, 59, 60–61, 63, 65, 92, 93
skill development (instrumentation) and, 17–19, 87–88, 97
Stella, 67–69
Context
　in constructivist leader development, 59–63
　in esthetics of leader persona, 87, 91–98
　fusion of social contexts, 94–98
　great-men theories of leadership and, 10–12
Conway, J., 8
Corporate culture, 15, 16, 95–96

Decision making
　as dynamic activity, 7
　motivation for involving others in, 9–10
　in participatory leadership, 7–8, 9–10
Dewey, John, x
Diffusion. See Identity diffusion
DuBrin, A. J., 8
Dynamic personality psychology, 25

Egalitarianism, 8–10
Elizabeth, 77–81
　career history, 77–78
　education history, 80–81
　family history, 78–80, 81, 84–85
　integrative leader identity, 81

Ellen, 82–84
    career history, 82
    education history, 82–84
    family history, 82
    identity congruence and, 97
    leader persona, 93
    proactive identity formation, 91
    religious faith, 82–84, 85, 91, 93–94
Embeddedness, 27
Erikson, E., 23, 28
Esthetics of leader persona
    convergence of conferred identity
        and professional constructions,
        88–89
    defined, 87–88
    instrumentation and, 97
    phenomenological epistemological
        processes and, 89–91, 94, 100
    social context and, 87, 91–98
Existential-phenomenological
    psychology, 25

Ferguson, K. E., 14
Foreclosure. *See* Identity foreclosure

Gardner, J. W., 10–12, 13
Gender
    identity development and, 22
    leadership style and, 3–4, 14–16
    socialization and, 1–2, 95
    work-related traits and, 15–16
Gilligan, Carol, ix, 24, 26, 28
Goldberger, N. R., 24
Great-men theories of leadership, 10–12
Greene, Maxine, ix–xi, 4, 14, 18–19

Helgesen, S., 15–16
Hunt, J., 13

Identity achievement, 23, 44–45, 46,
    48, 64–65
Identity congruence, 97
Identity development, 43–63. *See also*
    Identity status
    in constructivist leadership, x, 17–
        19, 27–28

fluid nature of identity and, 24
gender and, 22
identity formation versus
    construction of identity, 28
leader persona and, 21–27
meaning-making in, 25–26
meaning systems in, 25–26
moral judgments in, 24
nature of identity, 22
neo-Piagetian psychology and, 25,
    27
other-American cultures and, 24
proactive approach to, 90–91, 97–
    102
and psychosocial development, 21–
    22
as subconscious process, 23
theory of leader, 27–28
Identity diffusion, 24, 43, 44–45, 46, 47
Identity foreclosure, 23, 43, 44–45
Identity status, 22–27
    identity achievement, 23, 44, 46, 48,
        64–65
    identity diffusion, 24, 43, 44–45, 46,
        47
    identity foreclosure, 23, 43, 44–45
    moratorium, 24, 43, 45–46, 64–65
    nature of identity, 22
Identity status assessment, 28
Individuation, 26
Instrumentation (skill development),
    in constructivist leadership, 17–
    19, 87–88, 97
Irigaray, L., 24
Isabella, 73–77
    advocacy and, 75–76
    career history, 73, 74
    education history, 73
    family history, 73–74
    trusting relationships, 76, 85

Jacobson, S., 8
Jaggar, A., 14
Jago, A. G., 7–8, 9
Janeway, E., 15
Jefferson, Thomas, 11

Jessie, 69–73
  career history, 69–70
  compartmentalizing and, 70, 72
  confidentiality and trust, 70–71, 73, 85, 91
  genderization of leader persona, 71–72, 92
  leader persona, 92
Josselson, R., 22–27, 28, 43

Kegan, R., 17–18, 22, 25–28, 34, 40, 42, 49–50, 55
Kohlberg, L., 24
Kotter, J. P., 14
Kouzes, J., 8, 9, 12

Laidlaw, T. A., 24
Leader persona, 47–63
  of Anna, 48–50, 53–55, 59, 60, 65, 92
  defining features of, 48, 50–59
  of Ellen, 93
  esthetics of, 87–98, 100
  identity achievement status and, 48
  and identity development, 21–27
  of Jessie, 92
  of Odette, 55–61, 65
  proaction in design of, 90–91, 97–102
  and psychosocial development, 21–22
  of Samillia, 50–53, 59, 60–61, 65, 92, 93
Leadership
  attributes of, 12–13
  constructivist. *See* Constructivist leadership
  egalitarianism and, 8–10
  great-men theories of, 10–12
  mythical leaders, 10–12
  participatory, 7–8, 9–10
  power differentials and, 8–10
  task-related approach to, 6–8
  theory of identity development, 27–28
  trait theories of, 12, 13–14, 99
  transformational, 9

Leadership style
  gender and, 3–4, 14–16
  labeling of, 14
  prescriptive versus adaptive, 101
Leader studies, gender and, 3–4
Leland, C., 13, 16
Lincoln, Abraham, 11

Malmo, C., 24
Management
  participatory, 7–8, 9–10
  as responsibility of leadership, 7
Marcia, J. E., 22, 23, 24, 28, 46, 47
Matteson, D. R., 22
Maxcy, S., 8, 13–14
Meaning-making, 25–26
Meaning systems, 25–26
Messinger, R., 15
Mills, C. Wright, 8–9
Moral judgments, in identity development, 24
Moratorium, 24, 43, 45–46, 64–65
Morrison, A. M., 16
Mythical leaders, 10–12

New Leadership, The (Vroom & Jago), 7–8

Objective self, 65
Object relations, 25–27
Odden, A. R., 8
Odette, 36–40, 64
  career history, 37–40, 61
  education history, 37, 56, 61
  family history, 36–37, 38, 41–42, 56–57, 58, 59–60, 61, 62
  identity congruence and, 97
  leader persona, 55–61, 65
Organizations
  areas of divergence in, 96–97
  and congruence among individuals, 96
  culture of, 15, 16, 95–96
  functions of, 5
  hiring practices, 95–96
  leader importance and, 5–6, 97

Organizations (*continued*)
  procedures of, 96
  stability of, 5
Organizing principles
  defined, 66
  transcendent themes versus, 66
Orlofsky, J. L., 22

Participatory leadership, 7–8, 9–10
Personality
  dynamic personality psychology,
    25
  traits, 12–15, 99
Phenomenological epistemological
    processes, 89–91, 94, 100
Posner, B., 8, 9, 12
Power, 8–10, 92, 93–94
Proactive identity formation, 90–91,
    97–102
Professional development, 9
Psychosocial development, 21–22
Public persona, 47

Quality requirements, 9–10

Rosaldo, R., 16
Rothenberg, P., 14

Samillia, 30–33
  career history, 30
  education history, 30, 31–32, 50–52,
    61
  family history, 30–33, 40–41, 50, 52–
    53, 59, 61, 63
  leader persona, 50–53, 59, 60–61, 65,
    92, 93
  proactive identity formation, 90–91
Self-actualization, 25
Self-direction, 2
Self-knowledge, 17, 87–88
Self-mastery, 18–19

Self-perfection, 18–19
Self-study, 87–88, 89, 98, 99, 101–102
Skill development. *See*
    Instrumentation (skill
    development)
Socialization, 25
  case studies on, 16
  gender and, 1–2, 95
  in identity development, 27–28
  new corporate cultures and, 15
  of women as followers, 1–2
Stella, 67–69
Subjective self, 65
Subjugation, of women, 1–2

Tarule, J., 24
Task-related approach to leadership,
    6–8
Traits
  gender and, 15–16
  theories of leadership and, 12, 13–
    14, 99
Transcendent themes, 84–85
  and adaptation to leadership, 66
  defined, 66
  organizing principles versus, 66
Transformational leadership, 9
Truman, Harry, 11–12

Vroom, V. H., 7–8, 9

Washington, George, 11
Waterman, A. S., 22, 29, 42, 44
Watkins, G., 14
Weedon, C., 15
Weisstein, N., 14
Women's Ways of Knowing (Belenky
    et al.), x

Yekovich, F., 19
Yukl, G. A., 8

About the Author

Barbara K. Curry, Ed.D. is an Associate Professor in the College of Human Resources, Education, and Public Policy at the University of Delaware. She received her undergraduate degree from Franklin and Marshall College. She is a graduate of the University of Wisconsin-Madison, and received her doctorate from Harvard University. She is also a clinical social worker.